✳ ✳ ✳ KID ✳ ✳ ✳ SCIENTISTS

TRUE TALES OF CHILDHOOD FROM

SCIENCE SUPERSTARS

STORIES BY *DAVID STABLER*   ILLUSTRATIONS BY *ANOOSHA SYED*

Library of Congress Cataloging in Publication Number: 2017961241

ISBN: 978-1-68369-074-0

Printed in China

Typeset in Bell MT, Linowrite, and Bulldog
Dialogue font typeset by John Martz

Designed by Doogie Horner
Illustrations by Anoosha Syed
Production management by John J. McGurk

Quirk Books
215 Church Street
Philadelphia, PA 19106
quirkbooks.com

10 9 8 7 6 5 4 3 2

NEIL DEGRASSE TYSON   JANE GOODALL   ALBERT EINSTEIN   KATHERINE JOHNSON

✳ ✳ ✳ KID ✳ ✳ ✳ SCIENTISTS

TRUE TALES OF CHILDHOOD FROM

✳ **SCIENCE SUPERSTARS**

STORIES BY *DAVID STABLER* ILLUSTRATIONS BY *ANOOSHA SYED*

SALLY RIDE   MARIE CURIE   BENJAMIN FRANKLIN   NIKOLA TESLA

Table of Contents

Introduction

The painter Pablo Picasso once said that every child is an artist. It's equally true that every kid is a scientist. A scientist's job is to ask questions and seek answers, and who's better at that than a kid? Scientists begin by asking why, and then they find out the how.

You might not know all of the scientists in this book by name, but because of them, we know about gravity, DNA, dark matter, and black holes. We have electricity, calculus, and computer code, and we've walked on the moon. But before these scientists were making groundbreaking discoveries, they were just ordinary kids who were curious about the world around them.

Some loved gazing up at the night sky, like Neil deGrasse Tyson. He started a dog-walking business to save up money to buy his first telescope.

I HOPE THIS TELESCOPE IS WORTH IT!

And Vera Rubin, who discovered dark matter, used to stay up all night watching meteor showers from her bedroom window.

Some kids loved animals and nature, like Jane Goodall. Before she lived among the chimpanzees in Tanzania, she horrified her mother by keeping worms under her pillow.

As a child, George Washington Carver was also fascinated by the natural world. He loved the plants in his garden so much that he talked to them!

Others kids wanted to know how stuff worked, so they took things apart and built all kinds of contraptions. Long before he discovered gravity, Isaac Newton built a windmill that spun with the help of mice.

And Benjamin Franklin's very first invention was a pair of fins that allowed him to swim faster.

ASIDE FROM THE CONSTITUTION OR THE LIGHTNING ROD, I THINK THESE ARE MY GREATEST ACHIEVEMENT.

BENJAMIN FRANKLIN

· FRANKLIN FANTASTIC FINS ·

The things these kid scientists did for fun—whether star gazing, worm collecting, or toy building—ended up becoming the foundations of amazing discoveries. Playing, making messes, and asking lots of questions are some of the most important things a kid can do. They're also some of the best ways to develop a curious and scientific mind.

So who knows? Everyone starts out small, but if you work hard and dream big, you just might become the universe's next science superstar!

ONE

REACHING
FOR
THE STARS

CONSTELLATIONS, HOMEMADE TELESCOPES, AND PLANETARIUMS.

BEFORE THESE **KID SCIENTISTS** learned the secrets of *OUTER SPACE* (AND EVEN WENT THERE!), they loved gazing AT THE Night Sky.

Katherine Johnson

You Can Count on Me

The calculations of Katherine Johnson, a brilliant African American woman from West Virginia, helped put a man on the moon for the very first time. With support from her family and the guidance of her teachers, she was able to develop her extraordinary math skills. Despite facing racial predjudice, she became one of the heroines in humanity's race to the stars.

Long before her calculations helped the astronaut Neil Armstrong take his first steps across the moon, Katherine was counting the steps across her own front yard in White Sulphur Springs, West Virginia.

And that wasn't all she counted. "I counted everything," Katherine later recalled. She counted the steps from her front door to the road that ran past her house, the steps from her house to the church in the center of town, and the number of dishes, forks, and knives she had to wash after supper. "Anything that could be counted, I did," she said.

Katherine's love of counting only grew as she got older. She likely inherited her knack for numbers from her father, Joshua Coleman, a farmer who had left school after the sixth grade. Despite his lack of formal schooling, Joshua was a math genius. He could look at a tree and instantly tell you how many boards could be carved out of its wood, just by doing the calculations in his head.

Because he regretted leaving school at such a young age, Joshua always stressed the importance of education to his daughter and her three older siblings. Katherine's mother, Joylette, used to be a teacher, and she shared Joshua's enthusiasm for education. Whatever Katherine would achieve in life—and opportunities were few for African American girls when she was growing up in the 1920s—she knew it would begin in the classroom.

When still a toddler, Katherine started following her older brother to the two-room schoolhouse where he attended classes. At first, the teachers would not allow Katherine inside. But when they found out that she could already read—at an age when many kids were still learning to walk—they agreed to let her attend summer school.

Katherine made great progress. When it was time for her to begin elementary school, she skipped first grade and went straight into second grade—just before she turned six years old.

Katherine continued to make a good impression on her teachers. She raised her hand often to ask questions. But every once in a while, her teachers would turn away from the blackboard to see that Katherine was missing. They would find her in the classroom next door, where she was helping her older brother solve math problems.

Being smart is great, but it wasn't always easy for Katherine to be the brain in the family. Every night, she and her brother and two sisters would gather around the kitchen table to do their homework. After Katherine finished hers, she had to help her siblings finish theirs.

But being smart definitely had its advantages. When Katherine was about to start the fifth grade, she was permitted to jump ahead to sixth grade. She'd now skipped two grade levels, putting her one grade above her older brother. It seemed as if nothing could stop her progress.

But at the end of the school year, an uncertain future awaited. At that time, the state of West Virginia was segregated by race. White students in Katherine's town could continue on to high school, but there were no schools beyond the sixth grade for African American children like Katherine. It was expected that she would take a job as a servant or housekeeper.

Katherine's father had a different idea. He knew of a school in the town of Institute, 120 miles away, where Katherine could continue her education. It would cost a lot of money, but Joshua decided to send Katherine, her mother, and her three older siblings to Institute at the start of the next school year.

Joshua planned to move his family back home to White Sulphur Springs in time for summer break. To pay for all the travel back and forth, he took a second job as a janitor at the Greenbrier, a world-famous resort in their town.

Thanks to her family's sacrifice, Katherine was able to attend class without interruption. In fact, she got such good grades that she was able to start high school when she was just ten years old.

The teachers at Katherine's new school quickly recognized her capacity for learning. At the end of a long day in the classroom, the high school principal, Sherman H. Gus, would personally walk Katherine home. Along the way, he would point out the various constellations in the sky. This was Katherine's first experience with astronomy, the branch of science that would one day change her life.

When the school year ended, Katherine returned home. She took a job as a maid in the Greenbrier resort where her father worked. For the next few summers, she cleaned rooms, washed clothes, and catered to the wealthy and famous guests who passed through town.

One of these guests was an elegant French woman, a countess, who spent hours on the telephone talking to her friends in Paris. As she tidied up the countess's room, Katherine became transfixed by the sound of the French language.

When the countess noticed her maid listening to her conversations, she did not get angry. Instead, she took Katherine down to the Greenbrier's kitchen and ordered the chef to teach her how to speak French like a native. Before long, Katherine had learned the basics of the language.

TEACH HER FRENCH AND MAKE ME AN OMELETTE, PLEASE.

OUI M'DAME.

Despite having mastered math, started learning French, and been introduced to astronomy, Katherine was far from finished with her education. At the age of fourteen, she graduated from high school and earned a full scholarship to West Virginia State College.

Some kids might have been intimidated by the idea of going off to college at such a young age, but not

Katherine. She had grown up across the street from the school's campus and already knew most of her classmates. "I was the fresh kid in the freshman class and was treated no differently than anyone else," she said.

At West Virginia State, a historically black college, Katherine was fortunate to find teachers who understood what it was like to be the star pupil. One special teacher was Angie Turner King, one of the first African American women to earn an advanced degree in mathematics education. Like Katherine, Dr. King graduated from high school at age fourteen. She'd paid her way through college by waiting tables and washing dishes. She saw that she and Katherine had a lot in common.

During Katherine's sophomore year in college, she took a class taught by William Claytor, another African

American math pioneer. Dr. Claytor was a notoriously tough teacher. During class, he would furiously scribble equations on the chalkboard, and just as quickly erase them. Very few students could follow his lectures, but Katherine could.

After class one day, Dr. Claytor told Katherine that she would make a fine mathematician—and that was all she needed to hear. Katherine relished the challenge to excel in a field that offered so few opportunities for African American girls like her.

In 1937, at age eighteen, Katherine graduated from college with a degree in mathematics. Following her mother's example, she took a job as an elementary school teacher, married, and started a family. But when an opportunity arose to work as a mathematician for what would one day be called NASA, the National Aeronautics and Space Administration, Katherine leapt at the chance.

Katherine was part of a team of extraordinary African American women whose calculations helped NASA land the first astronaut on the moon in 1969. In 2015, in recognition of her contributions to America's space program, Katherine Johnson was awarded the U.S. Presidential Medal of Freedom.

Vera Rubin

Galaxy
Girl

Does the universe spin? If so, how fast? A lifelong fascination with the stars led future astronomer Vera Rubin to search for the answers to these questions, which she first contemplated while gazing through a homemade telescope in her childhood bedroom.

"**I became an astronomer** because of looking at the sky," Vera Rubin once said. More than books, more than teachers, it was her own sense of wonder that made Vera want to study the stars when she grew up. But before she could do that, she had to overcome the doubts of people on her journey to becoming one of the pioneering women in her field.

Vera Rubin was born Vera Florence Cooper on July 23, 1928, in Philadelphia, Pennsylvania. Her older sister, Ruth, was her closest friend. Vera's parents, Rose and Philip Cooper, worked for the Bell Telephone Company in Philadelphia. Rose calculated the mileage for private phone lines. Philip was an electrical engineer.

When she was a little girl, Vera's parents took her to the Morse School of Engineering at the University of Pennsylvania. Among the science exhibits on display was a device called the Van de Graaff Generator, a large aluminum ball mounted on a pedestal that generates static electricity. When Vera touched the ball, something unexpected happened: blue sparks shot out of it, and her hair stood on end!

A short time later, Vera visited another Philadelphia landmark, the Franklin Institute. This science museum and education center is named for Benjamin Franklin, one of the city's most famous residents. Vera was quickly dazzled by the Institute's walk-in kaleidoscope, a chamber of mirrors and colored lights that made her feel like she was on another planet.

Vera began to think about how the kaleidoscope worked. She decided to build her own using everyday household materials. When she got home, she searched the kitchen for a metal-tube and found an icing squeezer, which her mother used to frost cakes. Then Vera cut out three pieces of polished glass and glued them inside the cylinder; these would serve as the interior reflectors. When she held her creation up to the light—instant kaleidoscope! It wasn't the most spectacular light show she'd ever seen, but it worked.

IT'S ALMOST LIKE SEEING UNSEEN FORCES AT WORK IN THE UNIVERSE.

When Vera was ten years old, her family moved to Washington, D.C., for her father's job. Because space was limited in their new home, Vera and Ruth shared a bedroom and a double bed, which neither sister was happy about. To maintain their privacy, the girls drew an imaginary line down the center of the mattress. Vera's half of the bed faced the window. Beyond it was the northern sky.

From this "little windowed porch," as she called it, Vera could gaze up at the stars as they traced their course across the night sky. She became mesmerized by the constellations. She soon discovered that she could tell time by the movement of the stars and get a sense of the motion of the Earth as well.

Sometimes Vera saw meteors streaking through the inky blackness. During these "showers," caused by space rocks (meteroids) orbiting the Sun, she would stay up all night to observe the "shooting stars." Though her mother would scold her, for the most part Vera's parents allowed their daughter to pursue her new hobby.

While watching these spectacular celestial events, Vera memorized the path of each meteor trail. In the morning, she would draw a map and record her all of her observations.

After a few months of star-gazing with the naked eye, Vera decided that she needed a telescope to help her see more clearly. But telescopes are expensive. The most she could afford to buy was a telescope lens. The rest, she decided, she would have to build herself.

So Vera took a bus downtown and went to a store that sold linoleum flooring. She persuaded the manager to let her have one of the cardboard tubes the linoleum came rolled on. Then, with help from her dad, she fixed the lens to one end of the tube and looked through it. Her homemade telescope wasn't the best, but it was the best she could do with the materials on hand.

When Vera was fourteen, she asked her father to take her to a meeting of the local amateur astronomer club. There, she listened to a lecture by a famous astronomer named Harlow Shapley, who had used his observations of the motions of stars to estimate the size of the Milky Way galaxy. The lecture helped convince Vera that astronomy could be more than just a hobby; someday, it might be her career. From then on, she and her father attended the club's monthly meetings.

Vera also started borrowing astronomy books from the library and told a family friend, Goldie Goldberg, about her interest in the stars. One night, Goldie and her husband drove Vera and her sister to Virginia in their convertible car. With the car's roof open to the sky, they gazed up at the stars. Goldie taught Vera the names of the constellations, which Vera had never heard before: Ursa Major, Orion, Pegasus, and more.

Goldie also told Vera about her own girlhood science-related dreams. She had wanted to become an engineer, but at the time the University of Pennsylvania did not admit women to its engineering school, so she had to get a teaching degree instead. For the first time, Vera realized that there might be obstacles on her way to becoming an astronomer.

In high school, Vera continued to study astronomy any way she could. For her assignments, no matter what the subject, she tried to choose topics related to stars, space, or the universe. By the time she graduated, Vera knew exactly what she wanted to study in college. Her good grades earned her scholarships at several schools. Now she just had to decide which one to attend.

At first Vera considered Swarthmore College in Pennsylvania. But then the admissions officer there suggested that she take up a more "ladylike" career, such as painting the stars and planets instead of studying them. (After that experience, whenever someone placed an obstacle in Vera's way, she would call a family member and joke: "Have you ever thought about going into painting instead?")

Despite a lack of encouragement, Vera refused to let people's unfair and old-fashioned opinions about girls studying science stop her from pursuing her dream.

Vera also earned admission to Vassar, an all-women's college in New York. If she attended Vassar, she would have the opportunity to study with Maria Mitchell, America's most prominent female astronomer.

Vera thought Vassar was the right choice for her, but when she showed her high school physics teacher the acceptance letter, he simply dismissed her choice.

"As long as you stay away from science, you should do all right," he said.

WE'LL SEE ABOUT THAT!

FEH!

Vera didn't listen to his advice. In the fall of 1945, she left home for Vassar. Four years later, she became the only member of her class—male or female—to graduate with a degree in astronomy.

Vera moved back to Washington, D.C., with her husband, Bob Rubin, a chemistry student she had met on a summer break. She continued to work, teach, and study the stars until her death in 2016, at age 88. Among her many scientific breakthroughs, Vera developed a theory that galaxies spin the same way as solar systems do, and that an unseen force called "dark matter" governs the movements of the universe.

At first, many of Vera Rubin's ideas were considered controversial, but over time, other scientists have come to understand that she was right all along. "If astronomers are still using my data years from now, that's my greatest compliment," she once said. Whether or not they agree with her findings, astronomers the world over owe an enormous debt to a woman who opened the field to new voices and new ideas.

Sally Ride

Team Player

A natural athlete who nearly played tennis professionally, Sally Ride gave up sports in favor of science. Yet she never lost the will to win or the determination to be the best. An invaluable member of any team for which she was chosen, whether on the court or on the Space Shuttle, Sally made history by becoming the first American woman in space.

To be a pioneering female astronaut, you have to be mentally tough. Even when she was a baby, Sally Ride always knew what she wanted—or didn't want.

The first word Sally ever spoke was "no." No crib could hold her for long. She was always climbing out of them. No car seat could contain her. On family road trips, Sally was known to vault over the front seat and into the backseat, bellowing like the cartoon hero Mighty Mouse:

Sally was born in 1951 in Encino, California. Her mother, Carol, was the daughter of immigrants from the country of Norway who had built their fortune operating a chain of movie theaters and bowling alleys. Her father, Dale, was a college professor. Sally also had a younger sister, Karen, whom they called "Bear."

Dale and Carol Ride believed in letting their daughters explore the world without too many rules and restrictions. "Dale and I simply forgot to tell them that there were things they couldn't do," Carol Ride once said of their parenting style.

From an early age, Sally formed strong opinions about what she did and did not like to do. "If Sally was interested in a subject, she'd give it all her attention," her mother observed. "If she wasn't interested, she didn't give it her attention." One year, Carol tried to convince Sally to take piano lessons, but she gave up when her daughter clearly expressed her thoughts about playing the instrument:

Schoolwork also didn't hold Sally's attention. She was quiet and shy and disliked many of the subjects she was being taught. She found home economics to be especially tedious. There was nothing Sally found more disgusting than having to cook and eat a tuna casserole at eight o'clock in the morning!

One thing Sally did enjoy was reading. Her home was always filled with books, which she was devouring by the time she was five. Her favorite characters were Superman, Nancy Drew, and James Bond.

Sally also loved to read newspapers, especially the sports pages. Every morning, she would race her father down to the newsstand to pick up the latest copy of the *Los Angeles Times* so she could check the scores of the previous day's baseball games. She made crayon drawings of her favorite players and memorized all of their statistics.

When it came to sports, softball was Sally's favorite game, though she also liked football and soccer. She was always the first one selected for teams. Even boys who never picked girls changed their minds when they saw Sally play. One time, a boy tried to steal second base while Sally was pitching in a softball game. She wheeled around to pick him off and threw the ball so hard that it broke his nose.

The faster and more dangerous the sport, the more Sally liked it. She used to terrorize the neighborhood with her trick riding—first on her stroller, then on a tricycle, and finally bicycle. She also liked swimming, kayaking, skating, sledding, and riding ponies.

A different sort of adventure awaited Sally the year she turned nine. Her parents had decided to spend some time traveling across Europe. So they took Sally and Bear out of school, sold their house, and loaded all of their belongings onto a boat bound for the Netherlands. For the next year, the Rides drove around Europe in a white station wagon, with Sally acting as the navigator.

Sally and her sister visited several foreign countries and experienced their customs and cultures. At the end of each day, their parents would quiz them on what they had learned about the history of each place.

Sally took her first ferryboat ride in Denmark, built her first snowman in Austria, and got her first skiing lesson in the Swiss Alps. She started collecting stamps, filling four albums with sports-themed postage from different nations. She also ate Wiener schnitzel for the first time, which became her favorite meal. Sally kept a diary of her travels in a red leather notebook.

When she returned to California, Sally had learned so much that she was allowed to skip a grade. But then she was so far ahead that schoolwork bored her even more. She spent most of her classroom time distracted or staring into space, waiting for the bell to ring. One teacher labeled her a "clock watcher." Sally responded by saying that she wouldn't have to watch the clock if the lessons weren't so dull.

One thing that hadn't dulled during Sally's year abroad was her passion for sports. She began collecting baseball cards and once again started memorizing statistics. She even dreamed of one day playing short-stop for the Los Angeles Dodgers. However, when she switched her attention to football, her parents decided thay they had to intervene. Fearing the sport would be too dangerous, the Rides steered Sally toward tennis instead.

TENNIS IS SO MUCH SAFER THAN FOOTBALL.

Sally had played tennis during her European trip, so she didn't need much encouragement to take up the sport again with renewed enthusiasm. Soon she was spending all her free time in the driveway whacking a tennis ball against the garage door. She got so good so quickly that she began challenging adults to matches, which she won.

Sally's parents encouraged her to pursue tennis as a career. They even hired Alice Marble, a former world's number one women's tennis player, to give her private lessons. But Alice found Sally hard to control. "I'm fifty years old!" the sports legend would yell whenever twelve-year-old Sally blasted a shot past her.

"I had to duck like crazy," Alice later recalled. Even Sally's own mother had to stop playing with her because she could no longer keep up with Sally's atomic serves.

By the time she graduated from junior high, Sally was a nationally ranked amateur tennis player. She competed in tournaments across the country and even earned an athletic scholarship to the prestigious Westlake School for Girls in California. She amassed so many trophies that her mother began using them as soap dishes, candy trays, bookends, and paperweights.

Sally seemed bound for tennis superstardom—until she discovered another subject that began to compete with racquets and balls for her attention.

While attending Westlake, Sally took a course in physiology, which is the branch of biology that deals with living things and how they work. Sally quickly became fascinated by the class as well as by her teacher, Dr. Elizabeth Mommaerts.

Dr. Mommaerts introduced Sally to the scientific method, showing her how to perform experiments designed to prove or disprove theories about how organisms function.

At last Sally had found an academic subject that interested her as much as sports. Although she still followed the baseball box scores in the paper, she also took out a subscription to *Scientific American* magazine. Sally even asked her parents to buy her a telescope. At night, she would haul it out onto the front lawn and gaze up at her favorite constellation, Orion, or find Saturn's rings and point them out to her sister Bear.

Sally graduated from Westlake School as one of the top six students in her class. Then she faced a decision. She could continue to pursue tennis as a career, or she could devote herself to the study of science.

For a while, it seemed like tennis would win out. In college, Sally won a couple tennis championships and was even encouraged to turn professional by the tennis legend Billie Jean King.

In time, however, Sally realized that she was much better at science than she was at tennis. Sure, she could hit the ball hard, but she couldn't control it the way she could control an experiment in a laboratory. "Sally simply couldn't make the ball go just where she wanted it to," her mother said. "And Sally wouldn't settle for anything short of excellence in herself."

Eventually, Sally decided to give up competitive sports in favor of science. She still ran five miles a day, played rugby, and kept herself in top physical condition. But instead of winning tennis tournaments, she set her sights on a different goal: to become the United States' first female astronaut.

After earning an advanced degree in physics from Stanford University, Sally joined NASA in 1978 and rose steadily through the ranks. Just as on the playground, she was always among the first to be chosen whenever a team was created.

In 1983, Robert Crippen, mission commander for the Space Shuttle *Challenger*, asked Sally to join his crew for its second spaceflight. "I wanted a competent engineer who was cool under stress," Crippen said. "Sally had demonstrated that talent."

On June 18, 1983, Sally made the first of her two historic flights aboard *Challenger*. In all, she would spend more than 343 hours in space—more than any other woman at the time. The hard-hitting tennis prodigy turned science geek had picked her path to excellence—and rode it all the way to the stars.

Neil deGrasse Tyson

Look Up!

A make-believe trip into outer space turned an ordinary kid from the Bronx, New York, into a "star child" fascinated by moons, planets, and suns. That kid was Neil deGrasse Tyson. When he grew up, he brought that passion into the classroom and onto TV, becoming one of the world's most beloved science educators.

One starry night, in the autumn of 1957, the life of nine-year-old Neil deGrasse Tyson' changed forever. In the middle of a vast, domed amphitheater, the house lights dimmed and a booming voice announced:

WE ARE NOW IN THE UNIVERSE, AND HERE ARE THE STARS.

Comets streaked. Planets whirled. The moon waxed and the constellations appeared. A meteor vaporized, leaving a glowing trail in its wake. Seated in the dark, Neil was transfixed by a celestial light show the likes of which he had never seen.

This was Neil's first visit to a planetarium—the Hayden Planetarium in New York City—and his first encounter with the wonders of astronomy, the science of observing the sky.

When the lights rose, Neil realized that what he had just seen was only an amazing simulation projected

47

onto the theater's dome. Nevertheless, Neil's interest had been piqued, and his imagination fired. He decided then and there that he wanted to follow the stars for the rest of his life.

"The study of the universe would be my career," he said later, "and no force on Earth would stop me." From then on, whenever someone asked Neil what he wanted to be when he grew up, he proudly answered:

What seemed like a journey of a thousand light years was in fact just a short ride on a subway. Neil grew up in New York City, not far from the Hayden Planetarium, in the Castle Hill neighborhood of the Bronx. Later, he lived in Riverdale, in the fittingly named Skyview Apartments. Neil was the second of three children. Both his parents worked for the U.S. government.

Neil attended public school in New York City, and he did not distinguish himself in the classroom. One teacher complained on his report card that Neil should spend less time socializing and more time studying. "Your son laughs too loud," another remarked to Neil's mother during a parent-teacher conference.

But there was one teacher who saw potential in the young boy. She knew that Neil was interested in the stars and planets. So when she saw a newspaper ad for an astronomy class at the Hayden Planetarium, she cut it out and gave it to him.

The visit to the planetarium left Neil feeling that the universe was calling him to study it. But he still didn't know how. Then, one day, a friend named Phillip lent him a pair of binoculars.

"What am I supposed to do with these?" Neil wondered. "Look in people's windows?"

"No, silly," Phillip said. "Look up!"

And when Neil did, he saw a whole new world of wonder. That night, he used the binoculars to gaze up at the moon, mesmerized by the giant craters on its surface. Magnified by the binoculars, the moon was no longer just a circle in the sky—it was another world waiting to be explored.

Then, when Neil was eleven years old, his parents gave him his first telescope. It was small, but it seemed infinitely more powerful than the binoculars. Now Neil could see way past the moon to the planets beyond. Even far-off Saturn, whose majestic rings Neil had read about, seemed as close and as clear as his own outstretched hand.

I SEE THE MAN IN THE MOON!

ACTUALLY, I'M SATURN.

Neil could not get enough of his new hobby. In fact, his fascination with the universe soon outgrew the power of his beginner's telescope. He needed a larger instrument. But that would cost money, and his parents were not very wealthy.

Determined to have a more powerful telescope, Neil started a dog-walking service in his apartment building. In time, he had earned about half the money he needed, so his parents chipped in the rest.

Neil's new telescope was a thing of beauty: a five-foot-long tube that "looked like a cross between an artillery cannon and a grenade launcher," as Neil once described it. It came with a long extension cord that had to be plugged into an electrical outlet. Neil also bought a high-tech camera so he could take photographs of the things he saw in the sky.

One night, Neil brought his new telescope up to the

tar-covered roof of his building to test it out. A dentist who lived a few floors below let Neil plug in the cord inside his apartment. But a kid dragging around telescopes and cameras is bound to arouse suspicion. Another neighbor saw him, thought he was a burglar, and called the police.

Two officers quickly arrived and climbed up to the roof to make sure Neil wasn't up to no good. Neil assured them that his expedition was all in the interest of science. He encouraged the officers to peer through his telescope while he told them facts about the planets:

The officers had to agree. It really was pretty amazing.

Neil continued with his astronomical investigations for the next several years, eventually earning admission to the prestigious Bronx High School of Science. The summer he turned fifteen, Neil signed up for "space camp" at the Hayden Planetarium, where his adventure had begun. For the next month, Neil studied the stars and talked to scientists about the universe.

He also took a class with the planetarium's director, Mark Chartrand III, who became his first role model. Dr. Chartrand had a way of using humorous examples to make complex scientific ideas understandable to everyone. Neil received a certificate for completing the course, signed by Dr. Chartrand, which he still has to this day.

On returning home from camp, Neil was asked to give a talk to fifty adults. He told the audience all about what he'd learned at the planetarium. The sponsors of the talk paid Neil $50—more money than he had ever earned in a single day. "That's one hundred dog walks!" Neil marveled, thinking back to his old job.

DON'T TELL MY MOM
I'M EATING DESSERT
BEFORE DINNER.

Neil's presentation was so poised and polished that other astrophysicists started to take notice of him. Carl Sagan, a renowned astrophysicist and host of the TV show *Cosmos,* wrote a letter asking Neil to consider enrolling at Cornell University, where Sagan taught. Neil was highly impressed by Professor Sagan, whose shows and books made things like quarks and black holes sound as cool as comic books and video games.

In the end, Neil declined Professor Sagan's offer and decided to attend Harvard University. But their connection would one day be renewed. In 2015, several years after Carl Sagan died and Neil had succeeded him as America's best-known astrophysicist, TV producers asked Neil to host a new series of *Cosmos* programs.

In 1996, Neil returned to the place where his love for astrophysics began—the Hayden Planetarium—but now he was its director, a job he still has today. Neil revived Dr. Chartrand's tradition of presenting every astronomy student with a graduation-style diploma. He signed each one, as a way of honoring the scientists who came before him.

Like Dr. Chartrand and Professor Sagan, Neil uses humor and plain language to convey his enthusiasm for the science of astrophysics. That common touch has helped make Neil deGrasse Tyson one of the most popular and respected scientists in the world.

PART TWO

GREEN THUMBS AND ANIMAL LOVERS

SNAIL RACES,
WORM COLLECTIONS,
AND Secret Gardens.

Before they uncovered the
MYSTERIES
OF THE *   *
*   *
* NATURAL *
WORLD, *
THESE
Kid Scientists
just loved
playing outside.

George Washington Carver

The Plant Whisperer

As a boy, George Washington Carver talked to plants so he could learn their secrets. As an adult, this trailblazing African American botanist discovered hundreds of uses for such everyday crops as peanuts, sweet potatoes, and soybeans. His remarkable journey from enslavement to scientific immortality began in his very own secret garden.

George Washington Carver was born into enslavement in the mid-1860s, shortly before the end of the American Civil War. His parents, Mary and Giles, were enslaved by a frontiersman named Moses Carver, who had immigrated to the United States from Germany years earlier.

On a freezing cold night in the waning days of the war, infant George lay sleeping inside a small log house in the town of Diamond Grove, Missouri. Without warning, a band of bushwhackers sneaked into the nursery and snatched him from his cradle. This brazen kidnapping set in motion a chain of events that would change George's life forever.

The kidnappers were slave traders from Arkansas who objected to Moses Carver's support of the Union

Army. George's mother and sister Mary were also abducted in the same nighttime raid. His older brother Jim managed to escape into the woods.

The kidnappers fled back to Arkansas, where they planned to sell George to another slave owner. But Moses Carver hired a Union Army scout named John Bentley to track them down and bring them back.

A week later, Bentley returned to the Carver farm. He had located George, who had come down with a bad case of whooping cough and was close to death. George's mother and sister were never found. George was now without any parents. Back when he was just two weeks old, his father had been killed in a wagon accident.

I'M SORRY, MR. CARVER. I WAS ONLY ABLE TO FIND LITTLE GEORGE.

Nursed back to health by Moses Carver's wife, Susan, and reunited with his brother Jim, George faced an uncertain future. The Civil War had ended. Slavery was abolished, and all enslaved persons in Missouri were declared free. But George and his brother had no parents.

The Carvers decided to raise George and Jim as if they were their own children. "Aunt Susan," as George called Mrs. Carver, took care of him, but he still missed his mother. Sometimes George would sit beside her old spinning wheel in the Carver home and try hard to remember what she was like.

George felt the aftereffects of his bout with whooping cough for the rest of his life. He had difficulty breathing and was never as physically fit as Jim, who worked out in the fields alongside Moses. George spent most of his time indoors, where Aunt Susan taught him how to read and write using a Webster's elementary spelling book. She also showed him how to knit and crochet, using a needle he had fashioned from a turkey feather, and how to care for the plants and flowers that grew in the family garden.

The term "green thumb" could have been invented for George, who came to specialize in nursing diseased plants back to health. One time Jim found George in the garden, pressing his cheek against a sickly rose bush and murmuring words of comfort.

"What are you doing to those flowers?" his brother asked. To which George replied:

LOVING THEM!

"Anything will give up its secrets if you love it enough," George would later say.

George even started his own secret garden in the brush outside the Carver house so that he could pay closer attention to what he called his "floral beauties."

At first, people snickered at the little boy who talked to flowers, but his caring approach paid off. Before long the Carvers' neighbors started coming to George for help with their own gardens. They dubbed him the "Plant Doctor."

When George was well enough to venture outdoors on his own, he spent most of his free time in the woods, marveling at the abundant wildlife.

"I wanted to know the name of every stone and flower and insect and bird and beast," George recalled. "I wanted to know where it got its color, where it got its life." But there was just one problem: "There was no one to tell me," he said.

George tried to look things up in his spelling book, but it didn't have the answers he sought. So he started collecting specimens during his trips into the forest.

If he spotted a reptile or an insect that interested him, he scooped it up and carried it back to his bedroom for closer inspection.

The first time he showed up in the house with a frog in his pocket, Aunt Susan was furious. After that incident, she made George empty out his pockets before he could go inside the house.

Though his curiosity tested her patience, Aunt Susan could see that George had a special gift for the study of nature. She wanted to encourage him to continue his education, but at that time there were no public schools open to African American children in their town.

When George was eleven years old, the Carvers hired a private tutor to come to the farm and teach him. George was so inquisitive that he soon wore out his teacher with his constant questions. The next year, the Carvers decided to send George to a school for black children in the town of Neosho, ten miles away.

George couldn't wait to get started. Before he left, he stopped in his secret garden to say goodbye to his plants one last time. Then he made the journey by foot, carrying all his possessions—including his prized rock collection—wrapped up inside a handkerchief.

George arrived in Neosho well after dark. He was unable to find lodging, so when he came across a barn near the school, he bedded down for the night.

The barn was owned by Andrew and Mariah Watkins, an African American couple. They did not know that George was there. The next morning, when Mrs. Watkins went down to get some kindling, she discovered George curled up in the woodpile.

George introduced himself. "I'm Carver's George," he said, presenting himself as the property of Moses Carver.

"From now on," Mrs. Watkins replied, "you will call yourself George Carver."

Mrs. Watkins took an instant liking to the boy and agreed to let him stay as long as he was enrolled at the school in town. She and her husband became like parents to George. Every day when school let out, he would race to their house and help them with chores. In return, they gave him a room to sleep in and helped with his schoolwork. He called them Uncle Andy and Aunt Mariah.

Aunt Mariah worked as a midwife and knew all about herbs that were used in medicine. She encouraged

George to continue his study of plants, which he soon learned was a special branch of science called botany. "You must learn all you can," she told him. "Then go back out into the world and give your learning back to the people." George took those words to heart and never forgot them.

George also learned from Uncle Andy, who worked as a farmer and blacksmith, among other odd jobs. Both he and Mrs. Watkins encouraged George to believe in himself and to help others in the black community.

During George's stay with the Watkins family, he did well in school, went to church on Sundays, and picked up valuable skills, like how to cook and do the laundry. But eventually George felt that he had learned all he could in Neosho. It was time to move on.

One day, George heard that a group of people were planning to leave Neosho. They were headed to a town in Kansas that had a free school for African Americans. George saw his opportunity to better himself and asked if he could join them.

"If there's room for you in the wagon, you can come with us," they said.

George was only thirteen years old, but he had no doubt he could make enough room to fit. He ran home and started packing for another adventure.

Before he left Neosho, George decided to do one last thing as a way to thank Aunt Mariah. He gave her a garden of her very own. He found some wild orchids growing in the woods and planted them near the fence that ringed the house.

With that final job done, Gergoe climbed onto the wagon and headed off for the next stop on his journey.

Over the next few years, George moved several more times before earning a high school diploma from Minneapolis High School in Kansas. He faced many obstacles to completing his education because he was African American, and several colleges refused to admit him because of the color of his skin. Still, George persisted in his study of botany, eventually becoming the first black student to enroll at the Iowa State Agricultural College.

Heeding Mariah's advice to "give your learning back to the people," George used the knowledge he amassed to help poor farmers grow their own crops for food. He didn't invent peanut butter, as many people falsely believe, but he did preach the benefits of peanut farming wherever he went. George also invented hundreds of useful products made from peanuts, soybeans, pecans, and sweet potatoes.

Anyone else might have patented these inventions and become a millionaire, but George Washington Carver preferred to go down in history as a man who made a difference, not a man who made money. He even had this sentiment written on his tombstone:

He could have added fortune to fame,
but caring for neither,
he found happiness and honor in being helpful
to the world.

Rachel Carson

A Sense of Wonder

As an adult, this legendary biologist and nature writer warned about the dangers of pollution and its impact on the environment in her book *Silent Spring*. But Rachel Carson first developed her "sense of wonder" about the natural world as a girl exploring the woods around her family's farm in western Pennsylvania.

"I can remember no time when I didn't assume I was going to be a writer," Rachel Carson once said. "Also, I can remember no time when I wasn't interested in the out-of-doors and the whole world of nature."

Rachel Louise Carson was born on May 27, 1907, in Springdale, Pennsylvania, a small town on the Allegheny River. Her mother, Maria, was a piano teacher. Her father, Robert, was an insurance salesman.

The youngest of three children, Rachel grew up in a farmhouse surrounded by many acres of woods and apple orchards. As soon as Rachel learned to walk, her parents encouraged her to play outside.

Mrs. Carson especially took a keen interest in natural history. She considered the woodlands a vast laboratory where her children could learn all about plant and animal life.

Every morning, Rachel's mother woke her up early so she could listen to the birds singing outside her window. On the walk to school, Rachel would talk to the birds as if they were her neighbors.

Sometimes her mother would accompany her on walks through the woods and teach her the names of all the flowers, birds, and insects they encountered. Mrs. Carson even kept a diary to document their shared love of the outdoors.

On one of their walks together, Rachel noticed that the sky above the treeline was a sickly gray color. Her mother explained that this was because of ash being belched out of the steel mills downriver. Rachel began to understand that, along with her appreciation for the natural world came a responsibility to protect it— especially from pollution.

The more Rachel explored the world outside her window, the more curious she became. One day while she was rooting around in the yard, she discovered a fossilized seashell buried in the dirt. Rachel's mind teemed with questions: How old was it? How did it end up in a rural Pennsylvania field when the ocean was so far away? She was beginning to think like a scientist.

Natural processes fascinated Rachel. She started collecting caterpillars and cocoons so she could watch them metamorphose into moths and butterflies.

TIME TO SPREAD
YOUR WINGS!

Whenever Rachel came home with a new critter from one of her expeditions, her mother told her to return it where she had found it. Mrs. Carson strongly believed that creatures should be allowed to live freely in their natural habitats. Rachel was not even permitted to kill insects inside the house. Instead, she was instructed to catch them and let them go outside.

As much as she loved the world of nature, Rachel had one other great passion: reading. She liked stories about animals the best. Some of her favorite authors were Beatrix Potter, the creator of Peter Rabbit, and Gene Stratton-Porter, a pioneering female nature photographer who wrote a series of books on wildlife and birdwatching.

As she grew older, the seafaring novels of Herman Melville, Joseph Conrad, and Robert Louis Stevenson also captured Rachel's imagination.

Inspired by these writers, Rachel started dreaming up her own nature stories. Her first attempt was a ten-page book of animal drawings in crayon and colored pencil, each accompanied by a few lines of verse.

On the title page, she drew a picture of an elephant and inscribed it to her father:

This little book I've made for you my dear
I'll hope you'll like the pictures well
The animals that you'll find in here
About them all—I'll tell.

Many of the creatures pictured in the book were ones that Rachel had encountered on her walks through the woods. They included a mouse, a frog, a rabbit, and an owl. Other animals, such as a dog, a hen, a canary, and a fish, lived on the Carson family's farm.

When Rachel was ten years old, she decided to see if she could get one of her stories published. Every month the children's magazine *St. Nicholas* held a writing contest for kids. Winners were awarded gold badges, with silver badges given to the runners-up.

Rachel submitted her first story to the contest in May of 1918. "A Battle in the Clouds" recounted the exploits of a World War I flying ace in the skies over France. Her mother certified that "this story was written without assistance, by my little ten-year-old daughter, Rachel." The next day, Mr. Carson mailed the story off on his way to work.

A few months later, Rachel received a copy of *St. Nicholas* magazine with her story published in it, along with a silver badge for excellence. For the next year, she wrote and submitted action-packed war stories to the contest. Four of her tales were published, making her one of their star contributors.

When Rachel was fourteen years old, she made her first professional sale. The moment a $3 check arrived, Rachel wrote the words "first payment" on the envelope and tucked it away for safekeeping.

The next year, Rachel decided to switch subjects. Instead of writing about dogfights in the air or heroes of the Spanish-American War, she crafted a true account of her experiences searching for birds' nests in the woods near her house. In the story, "My Favorite Recreation," Rachel chronicled a day spent hiking on the trail with her dog Pal and "a lunchbox, a canteen, a notebook, and a camera" by her side. She listed all the birds that she and Pal discovered, from a hummingbird to a cuckoo.

St. Nicholas published "My Favorite Recreation" in its July 1922 issue. Rachel had become a professional nature writer at the age of fifteen.

That fall, Rachel put aside her pen—temporarily—to focus on the start of high school. She quickly won over her teachers with her good humor and excellent study habits. Four years later, she graduated at the top of her class. Inside her yearbook, her classmates printed a poem that praised her hard work and perfectionism. It read:

Rachel's like the mid-day sun
Always very bright
Never stops her studying
'til she gets it right.

For Rachel, "getting it right" meant teaching others about the importance of protecting the environment—something she continued to do for the rest of her life.

DWELL AMONG THE BEAUTIES AND MYSTERIES OF THE EARTH.

In her senior thesis, Rachel urged her classmates not to "recklessly squander our natural resources." Later, while working as a junior aquatic biologist at the U.S. Fish and Wildlife Service in the 1940s, she wrote a steady stream of newspaper and magazine articles about ocean life and other subjects. Eventually, she became so well known for her nature writing that she was able to devote herself to it full-time.

The publication in 1962 of her most famous book, *Silent Spring*, made Rachel Carson a household name. Even more important, the book helped inspire a world-wide environmental movement. But it was an article that Rachel wrote in 1956 that best captured the feelings of awe and amazement she first experienced as a kid scientist.

"A child's world is fresh and new and beautiful, full of wonder and excitement," Rachel wrote in her essay "Help Your Child to Wonder." In her writings, she stressed the importance of learning to appreciate the sights and sounds of the world around us, such as "the dawn chorus of the birds in spring." Just as her mother had taught her all those years ago.

Rachel also urged kids everywhere to pay attention to what the planet is trying to tell us. "Take time to listen and talk about the voices of the earth and what they mean—the majestic voice of thunder, the winds, the sound of surf."

Jane Goodall

Bringing the Outdoors In

Her study of chimpanzees in their natural habitat has made Jane Goodall one of the world's best-known and most-beloved scientists. But before she went to Africa to learn about apes, she learned all about the many different creatures who lived in her own backyard.

When Jane Goodall was a baby, a big blue dragonfly flew in through her nursery window. Her nanny chased it out of the room, but Baby Jane was still frightened by all the commotion.

A short time later, Jane's nanny was pushing her down the street in a baby carriage when yet another dragonfly—or perhaps it was the same one—swooped down on her. This time, Jane screamed in terror, so loudly that a man passing by jumped in and swatted the insect out of the air with his newspaper.

WAAAAAAAA!

DON'T WORRY, I'LL SAVE YOU!

Jane cried all the way back home. Seeing such a beautiful creature harmed felt worse to her than the fear of being stung. Though she was only an infant, Jane learned something about herself that day. "Being afraid of something," she explained later, "did not mean I wanted it killed."

There were lots of insects in the backyard garden of the London house where Jane grew up. In fact, some of Jane's earliest memories are of wandering through the garden in her mother's arms, exploring all the plants and creatures who lived there. By examining them, Jane learned not to be afraid of them. It was the beginning of her lifelong fascination with living things, which would make Jane Goodall one of the world's expert animal scientists.

When Jane was eighteen months old, her father gave her a toy chimpanzee. "His name is Jubilee," he told her, and then explained that he was named after a baby chimp that had just been born in the London Zoo. Some of the Goodalls' friends thought that the stuffed toy would scare Jane or give her nightmares. But Jubilee quickly became Jane's favorite toy. She took him with her wherever she went.

LAND HO, JUBILEE!

After Jane learned to walk, her curiosity about the natural world knew no boundaries. She began to wander through the garden on her own, digging up whatever creatures she could find.

One day, Jane's nanny discovered that Jane had unearthed a handful of worms and brought them back to her bedroom. The exasperated nanny alerted Jane's mother, but it didn't do any good. Jane refused to release the wriggling mass of crawling critters hiding underneath her pillow.

LOOK! AREN'T THEY CUTE?

Mrs. Goodall could have gotten angry with Jane, but instead she explained why it wasn't a good idea to keep earthworms in the house. She pointed out how hot and stuffy it must be for them, living under a pillow.

"They need the earth to live," Mrs. Goodall told her daughter. "If you keep them here, they'll die."

Jane didn't want that to happen, so she reluctantly agreed to take the earthworms back to their natural habitat. With her mother's help, she dug a hole in the back garden and placed them inside.

That wasn't the last time Jane would get a little too enthusiastic about her nature studies. A short time later, while visiting friends at their beach house, she became transfixed by sea snails that had washed up on the shore. She collected them in a bucket and, again, brought them back to her bedroom for closer examination.

When her mother came up to see what Jane was up to, she found sea snails crawling all over the place—across the floor, up and down the walls, behind the furniture. Everywhere!

It was the earthworm incident all over again . . .

And so, once again, Mrs. Goodall explained why the creatures that live in nature should not be moved.

"Those snails will die outside the sea," she said.

And, once again, Jane gathered them up and brought them back to the beach where they belonged.

The farm that belonged to Jane's grandparents would provide still more opportunities to observe the natural world in action. On a visit when she was four, Jane was tasked with collecting eggs laid by the hens. Where does the egg come out? Jane wondered as she gathered the eggs piled up in the straw.

To find out, the next day, Jane crawled inside the henhouse, crouched down in the corner, and waited for a hen to come in. Finally, a hen arrived, laid an egg, swished its feathers in triumph, and left.

An exultant Jane ran to tell her parents what she'd seen. But she didn't realize that she'd been gone for nearly four hours. She was surprised to find the entire household frantically searching for her. Even the police had been called in and a missing persons report filed.

"Wherever have you been?" Jane's mother asked.

"With a hen!" Jane replied, shaking straw from her hair.

When Jane's mother saw how excited her daughter was about this latest discovery, she calmed down and listened patiently as Jane told the story of her henhouse adventure.

AND THEN WHAT HAPPENS?

"Now I know how a hen lays an egg," Jane said proudly. From then on, Jane devoted almost all of her free time to observing animals and understanding their behavior.

But Jane's childhood was not completely idyllic. When she was five, war broke out between England and Germany. Her father enlisted in the army, and Jane and her family went to live with her grandmother on the southern coast of England. Her new home had a large garden filled with insects and trees, where she could watch birds make nests and squirrels gather nuts.

Around this time, Jane began caring for a large menagerie of pets that included, at various times, a cat named Pickles, a hamster, two guinea pigs called Gandhi and Jimmy, a canary named Peter, a tortoise named Johnny Walker, and a rambunctious black dog called Rusty. Jane and her sister Judy also kept a stable of snails whom they "raced" across the lawn, keeping track of the winners by painting tiny watercolor numbers on their shells.

With her sister and some friends, Jane formed a secret society, the Alligator Club, dedicated to the study of nature. She even founded a "museum," where she displayed the "specimens" that she collected—mostly seashells and toadstools—and charged admission to kids who wanted to check them out.

The centerpiece of the exhibit was a real human skeleton, assembled from bones saved by Jane's uncle during his days in medical school. Jane donated the proceeds from ticket sales to the local horse rescue charity.

ONE TICKET FOR THE CREEP SHOW, PLEASE.

See the amazing skeleton!

proceeds go to ♥ horse research ♥

When Jane was eight years old, she borrowed a copy of *The Story of Doctor Dolittle* by Hugh Lofting from the local library. The novel is about an Englishman in Africa who talks with animals, including gorillas, monkeys, and chimpanzees. The story captured Jane's imagination, and she read it again and again.

Another inspiration was Tarzan, a character in a series of novels written by Edgar Rice Burroughs. Jane spent hours in her backyard, sitting on a tree branch, reading the stories about a young boy raised by apes in Africa to Jubilee her stuffed chimp.

After watching a Tarzan movie, Jane developed a crush on the handsome "ape man" who swung through the trees on a vine, accompanied by Cheeta, his own chimpanzee companion. Although she had no idea how to make it happen, Jane decided that when she grew up, she would go to Africa, live among the apes like Tarzan, and communicate with animals like Dr. Doolittle.

At school, some people teased Jane about her dreams and ambitions. They believed that a girl should focus on finding a successful husband and not think about a scientific career. But Jane's mother encouraged her to ignore them. When Jane was old enough, she worked as a secretary, a waitress, and a film editor to save enough money for her first trip to Africa.

By the time she was twenty-three, Jane could finally afford to visit a friend who lived on a farm in Kenya. She booked passage on an ocean liner. It was her first visit to another continent.

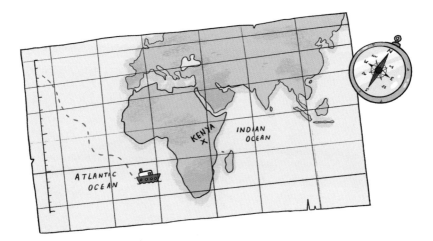

Africa was everything that Jane had imagined—and it was the place where all her dreams would come true. While in Kenya, she met Dr. Louis Leakey, a scientist known for his study of great apes. He offered Jane a job as his assistant, providing her first opportunity to observe chimpanzees in their natural habitat.

After working alongside Dr. Leakey for several years, Jane joined forces with two other trailblazing female scientists, the gorilla specialist Dian Fossey and the orangutan expert Birute Galdikas. Jane focused on chimps, becoming the world's foremost authority in her field. Together they became known as the Trimates.

In one of the many books she has written about her experiences, Jane Goodall credited her parents with teaching her to look at the natural world with a sense of wonder and curiosity instead of fear and hesitation. She thanked her father for giving her Jubilee, her first animal friend, who still sits on a chair in her home in England. And she thanked her mother for being "wise enough to nurture and encourage my love of living things and my passion for knowledge."

Temple Grandin

> Through an
> Animal's Eyes

I see the world an awful lot like a cow," explains Temple Grandin. Indeed, it was her love of cows and horses—as well as her ability to know what they are thinking and feeling—that inspired her to overcome the challenges posed by autism and become one of the world's best-known and best-loved animal scientists.

Mary Temple Grandin was born on August 29, 1947, to a well-to-do Boston family. She grew up attended to by maids and manservants. Because one of the family's maids was also named Mary, Mr. and Mrs. Grandin started calling their daughter by her middle name, Temple, instead.

By Temple's second birthday, her parents could sense that she was different. She didn't talk or laugh, and she often seemed lost in her own private world. Temple chewed puzzle pieces, stared at flapping flags, and twirled around in a circle for hours on end.

In those days, many people thought these behaviors indicated that a child was mentally ill. Some speculated that Temple might have epilepsy, a disorder that causes seizures. Today we recognize Temple's behavior as a sign of autism, a condition that affects how the brain works. Autism can make it difficult for people to communicate, understand behaviors, and process sensory information.

Temple explained what autism felt like to her:

"Sometimes I heard and understood and other times sounds or speech reached my brain like the unbearable noise of an onrushing freight train," she wrote. "I could understand what was being said, but I was unable to respond. Screaming and flapping my hands was my only way to communicate."

Concerned by their daughter's inability to speak, Temple's parents took her to the Boston Children's Hospital. She stayed overnight in the hospital, sleeping in a small bed surrounded by stuffed animals and dolls.

In the morning, the doctors performed a variety of tests, but could not determine the cause of her speech difficulty. They recommended that Temple see a speech therapist. Temple's parents also hired a nanny to play board games to keep her brain continuously occupied.

At age four, Temple finally began to talk. Around this same time, doctors were able to diagnose her with what we now call autism. Some of Temple's doctors recommended that she be sent to live in a mental hospital, but Temple's mother strongly opposed the idea. She decided to send her daughter to a private school for children with special needs.

At home, Mrs. Grandin worked hard to teach her daughter how to read. Every day for half an hour, she read aloud from an illustrated copy of *The Wizard of Oz*. Temple was enthralled by the pictures. She got so caught up in the story that soon she was reading entire paragraphs on her own. Before long, Temple was passing her reading tests with flying colors.

Temple also discovered that she had a talent for making things. After reading a book about inventors, she got ideas for projects she could create using everyday objects. She constructed a helicopter from a broken wooden airplane. When she wound the propeller, the toy flew straight up about a hundred feet into the air.

Temple also made bird-shaped paper kites, which she flew behind her bike from a thread. She experimented with bending the wings to make the kites fly higher. Thirty years later, airplane designers began using the same principle as Temple had tried, aiming to improve the performance of commercial airliners.

Just when it seemed as if Temple was progressing in her struggle to communicate, she entered junior high school. Beaver Country Day School was much larger than her elementary school had been. Instead of only thirteen students, her new school had as many as forty students in each class, which were led by a different teacher. The halls were noisy with banging lockers, which made Temple feel anxious and fearful.

Temple also encountered bullies. When she walked down the hallways in her new school, some students called her names because some autistic children have a habit of repeating words and phrases. Temple began to lash out to defend herself. She threw a book at a class-mate who taunted her and was expelled from school.

Following her expulsion, Temple's mother sent her to Mountain Country School, a private boarding school for children with behavioral problems in Rindge, New Hampshire. The environment at this new school was totally different from the one she had left behind.

Surrounded on all sides by acres of woods and streams, Mountain Country School contained a working dairy farm, sheep pens, and a stable with horses for the kids to ride. Temple would later learn that many of the horses there had behavioral problems, too.

LOOK AT ALL THE LOVELY ANIMALS.

"They were pretty, their legs were fine, but emotionally they were a mess," she wrote of the horses. "The school had nine horses altogether, and two of them couldn't be ridden at all. Half the horses in that barn had serious psychological problems."

Temple described one in particular, a horse named Lady. She said that was "a good horse when you rode her in the ring, but on the trail she would go berserk. She would rear, and constantly jump around and prance; you had to hold her back with the bridle or she'd bolt to the barn."

Then there was an unruly colt called Beauty. "You could ride Beauty, but he had very nasty habits like kicking and biting while you were in the saddle. He would swing his foot up and kick you in the leg or foot, or turn his head around and bite your knee. You had to watch out. Whenever you tried to mount Beauty he kicked and bit—you had both ends coming at you at the same time."

Worst of all was a beautiful light-brown filly named Goldie, who was perfectly well behaved as long as no one tried to ride her. Goldie was happy to let people pet and groom her, but she broke into a sweat and reared up in terror whenever anyone tried to sit on her back.

"There was no way to ride that horse," Temple said later. "It was all you could do just to stay in the saddle."

As a person with autism, Temple could identify with these fearful, anxious animals because she had often felt the same way. As she spent more time around them, Temple began to think that working with special needs animals like Goldie, Beauty, and Lady might just be her calling in life.

So she began spending every spare minute outside the classroom taking care of them. She cleaned their stables, groomed them, and rode them whenever she could. Nothing made her happier than whizzing around the barnyard atop one of her newfound friends.

One day Temple's mother gave her a special present: a brand-new saddle. It quickly became Temple's prized possession. She kept it with her at all times, bought saddle soap and leather conditioner, and spent hours alone in her dorm room washing and polishing it until it practically glowed.

A short time later, on a visit to her aunt's farm in Arizona, Temple watched as a group of cows were being loaded into a cattle chute to get their vaccination shots. At first, the baby calves were anxious and fearful. But they immediately calmed once they were inside the chute, where they were gently squeezed by the four walls that surrounded them.

HMMM, I WONDER IF I COULD TRY THAT?

Fascinated, Temple wondered if a "squeeze machine" would have the same effect on her. So she crawled inside and convinced her aunt to close the chute. In a matter of minutes, the gentle pressure made Temple feel calm, secure, and peaceful. She stayed inside the chute for half an hour. And it was there that she got the idea for her first scientific invention.

When she returned to school, Temple built her own "squeeze machine" for people like her who suffered from hypersensitivity to light and sound. She showed it to the school's psychologist, who did not understand what it was and told her to give up on the project.

But Temple knew she was on to something. She brought the device to her science teacher, Mr. Carlock, who instantly grasped its potential. Instead of trying to make her give up the squeeze machine, he offered ideas for improvements and even suggested a catchy new name for it:

HOW ABOUT WE CALL IT THE "HUG BOX"?

Mr. Carlock, who once worked for NASA, then gave Temple an important piece of advice, which she never forgot:

"He told me that if I wanted to find out why it relaxed me, I had to learn science," she wrote. "If I studied hard enough to get into college, I would be able to learn why pressure had a relaxing effect. Instead of taking my weird device away, he used it to motivate me to study, get good grades, and go to college."

Temple followed Mr. Carlock's advice. She worked hard, went to college, and applied the scientific method to gather evidence on the effects of her Hug Box on people and animals. She used the device for many years to relieve the symptoms of her autism.

The Hug Box was a breakthrough that made her name in the world of animal science and inspired the award-winning 2010 movie about her life. Temple Grandin used her new-found fame to advocate for the humane treatment of both people with autism and animals everywhere.

I COULDN'T HAVE DONE IT WITHOUT YOU.

MOO?

THREE

THE INVISIBLE FORCES

What goes up must come down—

*BUT*WHY?*

THESE **KID SCIENTISTS** were determined TO *UNRAVEL*

THE MYSTERIOUS AND OFTEN UNSEEN FORCES THAT CONTROL OUR UNIVERSE.

Isaac Newton

Underachiever No More

Isaac Newton likely always had the potential for great things deep inside. But he rarely applied himself to overcoming challenges and seemed destined for a life herding sheep on a farm. What it took was a confrontation with a schoolyard bully to get him to stop goofing off and start getting serious about science.

Isaac Newton was born on Christmas Day in 1642, in the small rural village of Woolsthorpe, in England. His father, also named Isaac Newton, had died three months earlier.

Born prematurely, baby Isaac was so small that his mother claimed he could fit inside a beer mug. She kept a tiny pillow underneath his head at all times to keep his airway elevated so he could breathe.

Many people in the village didn't believe that Isaac would survive infancy, but he surprised them all. He lived to the ripe old age of eighty-four, although he was much smaller than other boys while he was growing up.

Isaac was raised on his family's farm, known as Woolsthorpe Manor. When he was three years old, his mother remarried and left the home to live with her new husband in a village some miles away. She left Isaac behind in the care of his grandmother. Several of Isaac's other relatives lived nearby, but they never came to visit him.

With few friends and no visitors, Isaac entertained himself by drawing on the walls of his bedroom, which was upstairs in a drafty attic. He drew pictures of birds, ships, plants, and various geometric shapes. Once he had drawn an object to his satisfaction, he moved on to building a replica of it. Isaac spent his entire allowance on tools: saws, chisels, hatchets, and hammers. He spent hours alone in his room creating model sundials, windmills, and dollhouse furniture.

When Isaac was twelve, he moved to the town of Grantham, seven miles from Woolsthorpe, to attend school. Because his new school was far from home, Isaac boarded with a local family, the Clarks, who ran the village apothecary, or drug store. Mr. Clark often prepared medicines in his home, giving Isaac a chance to observe and learn the basic principles of chemistry. He also learned to use herbs to treat various ailments.

Isaac continued to draw, build things, and conduct experiments while he lived in Grantham. His sundial illustrations became so advanced that he could tell time just by observing the amount of sunlight in a room. He even constructed his own "water clock," a device that measured time by the steady dripping of water from one bowl to another.

By far Isaac's most ambitious do-it-yourself science project was his famous rodent-controlled windmill, or "mouse miller," as it came to be known. In Isaac's day, windmills were still a novelty, so when one was built near the edge of town, people came for miles to see it.

But Isaac was inspired to do more than just look at the new-fangled contraption. He studied every inch of it and created his own scale model. It was powered by a mouse on a tiny treadmill that was trying to reach a kernel of corn. Before long, the people of Grantham grew tired of gazing at the real windmill and came to see Isaac's mouse miller instead.

Not all of Isaac's experiments were as successful. For example, he designed a paper kite to which he attached a paper lantern lit by a candle. When the townspeople saw it streaking across the night sky, they assumed it was a comet crashing to earth and fled to their homes.

Isaac's inventions may have drawn the attention of his new neighbors, but they didn't win him any friends at school. He spent so much time daydreaming about what to make next that he neglected his schoolwork.

In his first year in Grantham, Isaac ranked 78th out of 80 students. He was bored with his studies and began acting out. He carved his name into a wooden window ledge in the classroom, lied to his grandmother about owning a crossbow, and once placed a pin inside another boy's hat so that it would stick him when he put it on.

On the playground, Isaac developed a reputation as a know-it-all, especially about science. When the boys at his school staged a jumping contest on a blustery day, Isaac won by correctly timing an incoming gust of wind and jumping at exactly the right moment. He expected his friends to be impressed by his mastery of what is now known as the principle of force, but they just thought he was showing off.

As Isaac grew more unpopular, he became a target for bullies. It was one such encounter that finally convinced him to change his ways and live up to his potential.

One day, the school's biggest bully, Arthur Storer, kicked Isaac in the stomach for no reason. Egged on by the other boys, Isaac challenged Arthur to a fight after class. The entire student body gathered to watch, expecting Arthur to score a quick knockout over the smaller, weaker boy.

But Isaac was determined to prevail. Calling on reserves of strength he scarcely knew he had, he soon gained the upper hand. Pulling Arthur along by his ears, he dragged him over to the school chapel building to deliver the finishing blow. That's when the crowd got bloodthirsty.

"Mash his nose into the side of the church wall!" urged the headmaster's son from the front of the throng of onlookers. When Isaac threatened to do so, Arthur gave in, promising that he would never bully anyone again.

It was a smashing victory, but instead of feeling triumphant, Isaac just felt ashamed. Violence, he knew, was not the solution to his problems. After all, he couldn't beat up everybody who tormented him. But he could beat them another way . . .

Then and there, Isaac decided to stop loafing around and start putting his intelligence to better use. He began to work harder in class, and in a short time, he became the top-ranked student in school.

Isaac's headmaster, Henry Stokes, took notice of his improved performance and urged him to continue his studies. When Isaac's mother wanted him to pursue farming, Headmaster Stokes convinced her that Isaac would be wasting his talents if he did not enroll in a university. Isaac won admittance to Trinity College, Cambridge, where he studied such legendary scientists as Johannes Kepler and Galileo.

In time, Isaac Newton would become their equal and build on many of their achievements. Today, he is remembered as the father of modern physics, the inventor of calculus, and the man who discovered the laws of gravity. The former small-fry grew up to be a giant in the world of science.

Marie Curie

A Secret Education

The world knows her by her French name, but Marie Curie was the daughter of proud Polish patriots who believed that learning was the key to independence. Long before her radiation research revolutionized science, she fought to get the education she deserved—no matter who tried to stop her.

Marie Curie discovered two new chemical elements—radium and polonium. But her most important achievement may have been the secret laboratory she kept hidden inside her house.

When she was just a toddler, Marie—then known as Manya Sklodowska—liked to play by herself in her father's study. One day, she noticed a strange object hanging on the wall. It was made of carved, curved brown wood and had a clock-like dial on an oval face. She later learned that it was called a barometer and was used to measure air pressure.

Across the room, she found a locked glass cabinet filled with test tubes, scales, mineral specimens, and something called a gold-leaf electroscope. As she stood on the tips of her toes to get a better look, her father entered the room. She asked:

WHAT IN THE WORLD ARE THESE CONTRAPTIONS?

"Physics apparatus," he told her.

Smiling, Manya sang the words back to him.

In time, she would come to understand that her father was a scientist, and these were the tools of his trade.

Wladyslaw Sklodowska was known as a well-read and knowledgeable man throughout his hometown of Warsaw, Poland. Manya and her four older siblings called him "the walking encyclopedia" because he was always teaching them something. He loved to entertain his children with informal lessons about science and history. When they went for a hike in the woods, he would point to the sky and explain about the stars. Sometimes the family would spend an entire afternoon re-enacting famous battles using blocks and toys.

But as educated as he was, Manya's father was not allowed to work as a scientist. At that time, in the late

1800s, Poland was ruled by the Russian Empire. The Russian authorities did not allow Polish citizens to work in laboratories. Mr. Sklodowska was forced to take a job as a school principal.

Wladyslaw and his wife, Bronislawa, were staunch patriots who believed their country should be free from Russian rule. They were convinced that an educated population was the best way for Poland to regain its independence. So when Manya became interested in science, they encouraged their daughter to pursue it.

Manya hoped to continue her education in grade school. But the schools in Warsaw were controlled by the Russians, who closely monitored every classroom. Students were allowed to speak only in Russian. And lessons in Polish history and culture were strictly forbidden.

Despite these restrictions, Manya did exceptionally well. "In spite of everything, I like school," she wrote in a letter to her best friend Kazia. "Perhaps you will make fun of me, but nevertheless I must tell you that I like it and even that I love it."

Manya's Polish teachers devised a scheme to fool the Russian authorities. When no one was looking, they handed out Polish textbooks and started teaching lessons on Polish heritage. When the inspector came to check on them, someone would sound a bell. That was the signal to pull out the Russian textbooks and hide the Polish ones. Since Manya was the star pupil and could read Russian fluently, she was often tasked with reciting the Russian lesson in front of the inspector.

When Manya was ten years old, her life took a turn for the worse. Her mother died of tuberculosis. And her father was fired from his principal's job and replaced by a Russian. To make ends meet, he turned their house into a boarding school. As many as twenty boys lived in the Sklodowska home. To accommodate them, Manya was forced to sleep on a couch in the dining room. She woke up at six every morning to cook breakfast for the hungry throng.

When she was fifteen, Manya graduated from high school with high honors. She was awarded a gold medal for being the best in her class. But between studying, taking care of her father, and doing the housekeeping, she was exhausted. Her father decided to send her to stay with an aunt and uncle at their house in the country for some much-needed rest.

The planned short vacation turned into a long, leisurely year during which Manya lived a completely carefree life for the first time. With no chores to do, no lessons to learn, and no Russian officials looking over her shoulder, she devoted herself to the simple pleasures of country living: fishing, boating, swimming, and riding horses.

Instead of her usual math and science textbooks, Manya spent her time reading Polish novels. "I can't believe geometry or algebra ever existed," she wrote to her friend Kazia. "I have completely forgotten them." Clad in a brand-new pair of shoes, she danced the night away with her cousins at a fancy ball. When the weather turned cold, she went on sleigh rides in the snow-covered countryside.

Manya also discovered her talent for practical jokes. One of her relatives was a neat freak, so Manya and her cousins pounded nails into the rafters and hung all his furniture upside down. Then they hid nearby until he returned home. The relative was shocked to discover all his possessions—including his shoes—suspended from the ceiling.

EVEN MY SHOES?!?

The year away from her troubles was just what she needed. Manya returned home feeling refreshed and rejuvenated—ready to continue her education in college. But there was just one catch: The Russian Ministry of Education had issued a decree to every university in Poland, banning women from enrolling.

Fortunately, Manya was used to pulling the wool over the eyes of Russian authorities. She heard about a secret illegal school where Polish women could take college courses in private homes. The teachers were well-read historians, philosophers, and scientists, all of whom believed in the cause of Polish independence. To avoid detection, classes were held after dark in changing locations. It was called the "Floating University."

For the next few years, Manya worked as a tutor and children's governess during the day, and attended the Floating University at night. When she got home, if she had time, she read science and mathematics textbooks. On weekends, she conducted experiments in physics and chemistry.

Eventually, Manya had learned enough—and earned enough money—to leave Poland. She moved to Paris, France, where she was able to continue her university studies without having to hide from Russian authorities.

In Paris, she earned two advanced degrees and began to answer to the French version of her name, Marie. She also met and married the French physicist Pierre Curie. Together they made numerous scientific breakthroughs and were awarded the Nobel Prize for physics in 1903. Marie earned a second Nobel Prize, for chemistry, in 1911, making her the first woman to win a Nobel Prize and the first person to win two Nobel Prizes.

Yet no matter how much she accomplished, or by what name people called her, Marie Curie never lost her Polish identity. For the rest of her life, she signed her name "M. Sklodowska Curie." She also made sure to teach her two daughters to speak Polish as well as French. And when she discovered a new element in 1898, she named it polonium, after the country where she was born.

POLONIUM IS LIKE MY HOMELAND: LUMINOUS AND FULL OF ENERGY!

Albert Einstein

Bad Albert

Today we consider Albert Einstein as the most creative scientific mind of the 20th century. But he began life as a slow learner and a poor student with a rebellious streak that nearly got him kicked out of school. His long journey from bad to brilliant wasn't quite as easy as $E=mc^2$.

From the day he was born, in 1879, Albert Einstein was a huge disappointment to his entire family.

"Much too fat, much too fat!" exclaimed his grandmother the first time she saw him. Albert's mother, Pauline Einstein, was dismayed by the size and shape of her baby's head. It seemed much too large and oddly pointy. She wondered if her newborn might be some kind of alien monstrosity.

Eventually, Albert's family relaxed a bit about the new addition. A doctor managed to convince his mother that her son's noggin was perfectly normal. And after a chubby infancy, he began to grow and develop at the same rate as other children, with one exception. Albert was very slow to learn how to speak.

Albert's parents consulted a specialist to find out if he might have a learning disability. In those days, many people falsely thought that if a person were quiet, there must be something wrong with them. The Einsteins' maid came up with a mean nickname for Albert: she called him *der Depperte,* German for "the dopey one."

According to family legend, Albert broke his long silence one night at the dinner table by proclaiming:

THE SOUP IS TOO HOT!

I'M SO PROUD OF YOU.

BRAVO, SON!

YAY!

Greatly relieved, his parents asked why he had never spoken up. "Because up to now everything was in order!" Albert answered.

Even after he began speaking, Albert rarely said what people expected him to say. For example, when he was two years old, he laid eyes on his little sister Maja for the first time. He thought she was a toy and asked,

"Where does it have its small wheels?" Once he realized that his sister was not some sort of motorized contraption, Albert became Maja's best friend, and she became his biggest supporter.

YOU'RE NOT NEARLY AS FAST AS MY TOY CARS.

Maja would often find her brother off by himself, sounding out words and phrases under his breath. He was practicing until he felt confident enough to say them aloud. "Every sentence he uttered," Maja later recalled, "no matter how routine, he repeated to himself softly, moving his lips." Albert did this routine until he was nine years old.

Albert spent most of his childhood in the German city of Munich, where his father, Hermann, ran a small electrical equipment company with his brother Jakob. As a young boy, Albert was prone to temper tantrums, perhaps because of his speech difficulties.

When his anger boiled over, his face would turn a ghostly white. Sometimes he even took his frustrations out on his sister. One time, in one of his rages, he hurled a bowling bowl at Maja. Another time, he hit her on the head with a garden hoe.

ENERGY EQUALS A MESS TIMES CHAOS SQUARED!

By the time he started school, Albert had learned to control his temper. But he never got along with his teachers, and he developed a reputation as a difficult student. He spent most of his time in class staring off into space, thinking about anything but the topic that was being taught.

Albert especially liked to confound his teachers. He would ask them complicated questions that he knew they couldn't answer. His attitude and disobedience led one of his instructors to declare that Albert would never amount to much in life.

Albert's mother hoped that music would provide a positive outlet for her son. So when Albert was five years old, she hired a tutor to give him violin lessons. Albert found the endless drills so tedious that he threw a chair at his teacher, who proceeded to run out of the house in tears.

Later that year, Albert became sick and had to stay in bed for several weeks. To keep him occupied while he recovered, his father gave him a compass. The navigational instrument captured his imagination in a way the musical instrument had not. Albert was mesmerized by the way the compass needle always pointed north, no matter which way he aimed it. His father explained that it was because of an invisible force called magnetism.

Albert was fascinated to learn that there was an unseen power in the world whose influence could be observed and measured. "This experience made a deep and lasting impression on me," he later said. "Something deeply hidden had to be behind things." For the rest of his life, Albert devoted himself to studying these mysterious forces.

At last Albert had found a subject that interested him. Now all he needed was a language to help him understand scientific properties and communicate his ideas to others. He found that language in mathematics.

During a visit to the Einsteins' home, Albert's Uncle Jakob noticed that his nephew liked to solve math problems in his spare time. Though Albert was still young for such advanced work, Jakob introduced him to the branch of mathematics called algebra. Together they worked on tricky algebra problems as if they were playing a game. Whenever Albert solved a problem before his Uncle Jakob—which was often—he would let out a victory yell.

Another visitor to the Einstein household also took note of Albert's love of numbers. Max Talmey, a young medical student, ate dinner with the Einstein family every Thursday evening. On one of his visits, Max gave a geometry book to Albert. Before long, Albert had plowed through the entire book, solving every problem.

Suddenly Albert had a new hobby: the world of shapes and angles. Each Thursday when Max came over, Albert would show him his completed work. After geometry, Albert moved on to bigger and better (and more complex) things: calculus.

Even though Max was ten years older than Albert, he soon found himself surpassed by his ten-year-old pupil. "The flight of his mathematical genius was so high that I could no longer follow," Max later confessed. He started lending Albert books on other subjects, such as physics and philosophy, to occupy the boy's rapidly growing mind.

The more Albert learned, the more he wanted to learn. He even returned to music. Now that he understood how math and music were related, notes and scales no longer seemed so boring. He began taking violin lessons again (though with a new teacher).

In 1893, the year Albert turned fourteen, his father and uncle decided to move their electrical equipment business to Italy in search of steadier work. Albert's parents left him behind in Munich to finish his studies.

But after six months of sitting in stuffy classrooms, listening to instructors drone on about subjects that didn't interest him, Albert was feeling restless. He missed his family and wnated to live in Italy, where the weather was warm all year long. So he hatched a plan to get out of Germany once and for all.

Albert managed to convince a doctor to write a note declaring that he had to move for health reasons. Then he persuaded his math teacher to allow him to withdraw from school because he had learned all he could. Truth be told, the teachers at Albert's school were tired of dealing with him and were happy to see him go. Albert was glad to be moving on as well.

Soon, Albert rejoined his family in Italy. Although it took a while, he completed his secondary education and went to university in Switzerland. There, at last, he was free to let his mind wander and pursue his favorite subjects. This led to several important breakthroughs that would one day earn him the Nobel Prize in physics, among many other honors.

The one-time poor student eventually became a teacher, spending many years as a professor in the United States, teaching at Princeton University. But no walls could contain Albert Einstein—he believed the entire world was his classroom. Wisdom, he once said, "is not a product of schooling but of the lifelong attempt to acquire it."

THANKS FOR THE COMPASS, DAD.

Rosalind Franklin

> An Inquiring
> Mind

Rosalind Franklin's research helped unlock the secret of life on Earth: the structure of DNA. But because of her gender, she was never given proper credit for her discoveries. Only in recent years have people begun to recognize the accomplishments of this proud "girl geek," whose brilliance was apparent from her childhood days.

Some people are born to challenge authority. Even as a young girl, Rosalind Franklin was always asking tough questions. When her mother first started teaching her about religion, Rosalind pressed her for proof that God was real. "Of course he's real," her mother replied, doing her best to provide the answers her daughter was seeking. But Rosalind remained skeptical.

"Well anyhow," Rosalind asked, "how do you know he isn't a she?"

Muriel Franklin probably wasn't surprised by her daughter's questions. Rosalind came from a long line of rebels. In the early 20th century, her Aunt Alice was a leader of the British Suffragist movement. Her Uncle Hugh once started a fight with Winston Churchill, Britain's future prime minister, because Churchill didn't think women should be allowed to vote.

Rosalind's Aunt Mamie, who was living in Jerusalem, was notorious for driving her car around town at all hours—an absolute no-no for women in her day.

In fact, it was Mamie who first took note of her favorite niece's extraordinary ability with numbers. "Rosalind is alarmingly clever," she once wrote. "She spends all her time doing arithmetic for pleasure, and invariably gets her sums right."

But it was from her father that Rosalind inherited her love of math and science. As a young man, Ellis Franklin hoped to become a physicist. Instead, after serving in the British army during World War I and marrying, he took a high-paying job in his father's bank. At night, he taught science classes at a school for people who could not afford a university education.

A true do-it-yourselfer, Rosalind preferred making real things to playing pretend (although she did have a pair of imaginary friends, named Tinker and Duster). Her hobbies were sewing, carpentry, and photography. Rosalind's mother was her partner for many of these pursuits. They spent hours together in the darkroom, developing pictures by hand. The process was slow and tedious, but for Rosalind, that was why it was satisfying.

"It makes me feel all squidgy inside," Rosalind would say as a new image gradually came into focus.

Puzzles and crosswords also appealed to Rosalind's logical mind. She loved challenging her father at word games and took special pride in defeating her older brother David. As the oldest girl in her family, Rosalind was eager to prove that she could compete on the same level as her three brothers.

Once, David showed off his foreign language skills by writing his sister a letter in French. Rosalind was green with envy. She immediately had the letter translated into English so she could read what it said.

As strong as she was mentally, Rosalind was frail physically. She was sick a lot, and at one point she caught a serious infection that had her parents fearing for her life. They confined their daughter to bed until she recovered. Rosalind resented that her brothers never had to face such restrictions when they were ill.

YOU CAN'T KEEP ME DOWN JUST BECAUSE I'M A GIRL!

It would not be the last time Rosalind believed that she was being treated unfairly just because she was a girl.

To improve her health, Rosalind spent more and more time outdoors. On weekends, she would stay at her grandparents' country house, a large estate with two tennis courts, a croquet lawn, and acres of farmland filled with cows, chickens, and turkeys.

One day Rosalind went down to the pond to catch tadpoles. Instead came away with a newt—a tiny lizard—which she kept inside a jar. "We do not know what to feed him," she wrote to her family. "Monica [her cousin] says worms and raw meat, but he does not eat much."

NEWTON, YOU HAVE TO EAT IF YOU WANT TO GET BIG.

When Rosalind was nine years old, her parents sent her to Lindores School for Young Ladies, a boarding school by the sea. Mr. and Mrs. Franklin thought the salty air might be good for Rosalind's health. After two years away from home, Rosalind returned to London and attended St. Paul's Girls' School, one of the only girls' schools in the city that taught physics and chemistry.

At St. Paul's, Rosalind excelled not only in science but in Latin, German, and French as well. She played hockey, cricket, and tennis, and joined the Debating Society. The only subject she was unable to master was music. She was so tone deaf that her music teacher asked her mother if she had a hearing problem.

By age fifteen, Rosalind knew that she wanted to pursue a career in science. She graduated from high school with high honors and set her sights on college. When she passed the admission exam to Cambridge University, she seemed to be on her way. But there was just one problem: Her father refused to pay the tuition. Even though his own dream of becoming a scientist had been thwarted, Ellis Franklin did not approve of university education for women.

Fortunately, Rosalind had powerful allies on her side. One of her wealthy aunts volunteered to pay for her school, while her mother worked to wear down her father's resistance. Eventually, Mr. Franklin gave in.

After completing college, Rosalind Franklin went on to a successful career as a biophysicist. Her research led to the discovery of the structure of DNA, the building block of all life on earth. Although she never received the credit she deserved for this breakthrough during her lifetime, historians now recognize the invaluable contribution she made to one of the most important scientific achievements the world has ever known.

PART

FOUR

DO IT
YOURSELF

MODEL AIRPLANES, SWIM FINS,

** AND A **

Bug-Powered WHEEL.

BEFORE THESE

KID SCIENTISTS

BECAME

BRILLIANT INVENTORS, they practiced by building THEIR VERY OWN

TOYS.

Benjamin Franklin

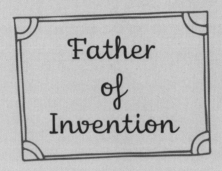

Father of Invention

One of America's best-known Founding Fathers was also one of its most brilliant inventors. Ben Franklin invented bifocals and the lightning rod, but long before those, he created the Fantastic Franklin Swim Fins. The fins never did catch on, but they proved that, even as a kid, Franklin knew that the best way to solve an old problem was to come up with a new solution.

Ben Franklin loved the water. From the window of his house in Boston, Massachusetts, he could gaze upon the thousands of tall-masted ships passing through the harbor, dreaming of one day working as a hired sailor.

But Ben's father, Josiah Franklin, had other ideas. He wanted Ben to be a minister. Not only that, but the Franklins had already lost two sons to water: Josiah Junior had been lost at sea, and Ebenezer drowned in a tub.

Josiah, a chandler, had plenty of work to keep Ben from daydreaming about his sailing future. When he wasn't in school, Ben had to help his father make soap and candles. His job was to skim the scum off the steaming vats of animal fat. It was filthy, smelly work that made Ben's clothes stink.

A BATH IN THE CHARLES RIVER SURE SOUNDS GOOD RIGHT ABOUT NOW . . .

But Ben was inventive, and he found small ways to rebel against his father's wishes. One day, he convinced some friends to build a makeshift wharf using stones they'd pilfered from a nearby construction site. The next morning, the workmen arrived and realized their stones had been taken. Ben and his friends were later punished for stealing.

If he couldn't sail the sea, Ben decided that at least he could learn to swim. He discovered a book called *The Art of Swimming*. It contained instructions for various techniques, along with arguments about the importance of swimming. "A good swimmer may not only preserve his own life, but several others also," the text stated. The author went on to list situations when being a good swimmer might come in handy.

- When being pursued by an enemy and meeting a river in one's way
- If an open vessel on the sea in a storm is sinking, or has lost its anchors and cables
- In case of a shipwreck

Ben studied the book, practicing all the exercises in the Charles River. He quickly became an expert swimmer and began teaching his friends his finest moves.

Even though he mastered all the basic strokes, Ben was still dissatisfied. He wanted to swim faster. To do so, he reasoned that he would need to re-create the paddling power of creatures like penguins, seals, sea lions, turtles, and sea otters. But how?

Using found materials, Ben constructed a pair of artificial fins. Shaped like a painter's palette, they had holes for his thumbs to keep them attached. When his prototype was completed, Ben tested them out. By pushing the edge of the fins forward, then pulling the flat surface behind him, he swam much faster.

Just as any scientist would do, Ben reviewed his experiment to figure out what worked and what needed to be improved. He declared the great swim-fin trial a success, but with some reservations.

For one thing, paddling this way quickly tired out his wrists. So Ben figured out a less strenuous way to move through the water. The next time he went for a swim, he brought along a paper kite. He tied its string to a stake, allowing the kite to float high in the sky. Then he lay on his back and allowed the kite to draw him downstream.

AHH, WHAT AN AGREEABLE WAY TO TRAVEL.

To slow down, Ben simply sat up and adjusted the height of the kite. When he reached the other side, his clothes were waiting for him. He'd had the foresight to hire another boy to carry them over there for him.

Ben's feats of aquatic prowess extended beyond his homeland. As a young man, he spent two years working as a printer in London. One day, some friends challenged him to swim a stretch of the Thames River, from Chelsea to Blackfriars. Ben immediately took off his clothes, jumped into the water, and swam three and a half miles, performing tricks along the way, to the amazement of onlookers.

Ben returned to the American colonies in 1726, at the age of 20, and settled in Philadelphia. In his new city, he proposed that all schools in the Commonwealth of Pennsylvania have swimming programs. Later, after he had earned renown for his electrical experiments and other achievements, Ben wrote a letter to a friend extolling the virtues of swimming.

"Learn fairly to swim," he advised, "as I wish all men were taught to do in their youth; they would, on many occurrences, be the safer for having that skill, to say nothing of the enjoyment in so delightful and wholesome an exercise."

For his efforts to promote swimming and water safety, Benjamin Franklin was inducted into the International Swimming Hall of Fame and the Pennsylvania Swimming Hall of Fame in 1968. These are just two of the fourteen such institutions that have honored this accomplished statesman, scientist, inventor, and icon.

ASIDE FROM THE CONSTITUTION AND THE LIGHTNING ROD, I THINK THESE ARE MY GREATEST ACHIEVEMENT.

Ada Lovelace

Poetical Scientist

The world's first computer programmer was the daughter of a stern math whiz and a flamboyant poet. By taking inspiration from both her father's grand imagination and her mother's logical mind, Ada Lovelace was able to dream of things that never were—and then make them a reality.

Augusta Ada Byron, the future Countess of Lovelace, was born into a wealthy and distinguished family. Her father was Lord Byron, one of England's greatest poets of the Romantic era and a notorious playboy. It was said that he was so good-looking that any woman who laid eyes on him fell instantly in love—and many did. He became legendary as a man who was "mad, bad, and dangerous to know."

Ada's mother, Annabella Milbanke, known as Lady Byron, was a prim and reserved woman who preferred solving math puzzles to romantic misadventures. Lord Byron nicknamed her "the Princess of Parallelograms" for her amazing geometry skills.

When Ada was still a baby, her parents separated. Lady Byron was fed up with her husband's wicked ways and wanted their child to grow up in a more stable home. She took Ada to live with her at her parents' home in Leicestershire. Lord Byron left to travel the European continent, fight in the Greek civil war, and write epic poems about love and piracy.

From then on, Ada's parents communicated only by letter.

Lady Byron was terrified that Ada would grow up to be as "mad and bad" as her father, so she vowed to raise her to follow her example and not Lord Byron's. "I hope the gods have made her anything save poetical," Lady Byron once said. "It is enough to have one such fool in the family."

Accordingly, Lady Byron taught Ada math and science, but forbade her from reading poetry, which she believed was bad for one's character. Ada also received lessons in history, geography, sewing, and shorthand.

Lady Byron was a stern taskmaster. When Ada got something right, her mother awarded her a paper ticket. When she got something wrong, daydreamed, or otherwise misbehaved, a ticket was taken away. If she failed to meet her mother's expectations, Ada was sent to sit in a closet by herself.

Lady Byron often left Ada alone for months at a time while she traveled to Europe, seeking cures for her various ailments. When she was away, a series of tutors and governesses took over Ada's education. Ada had few friends, and she spent much of her time lying in bed reading or playing with her pet cat, Madame Puff.

Despite her mother's best efforts, Ada never lost the poetic spirit she had inherited from her father. When she was five, Lord Byron sent Ada a locket of his hair to carry with her. In return, she sent him a portrait of her, which he kept until he died four years later.

As she grew older, Ada thought about how she might fuse her father's fiery imagination with the mathematical knowledge she learned from her mother. She even came up with a term, "poetical science," to describe what she was aiming for. Ada increasingly looked for playful ways to use science to solve problems.

One day, when Ada was twelve, she caught Madame Puff inside the chimney, munching on a dead bird that she had caught.

Ada was disgusted, but also inspired by the unusual shape of the bird's skeleton. It fascinated her to see how its wings worked, and the way its unique physical form allowed it to sail through the sky.

However, Ada wasn't merely smitten with the idea of learning how birds flew. She wanted to build a flying machine of her own. For more than a year, she spent all her free time studying the anatomy of the birds that Puff dragged in from the garden.

When she had mastered the science of flight, Ada started collecting materials she thought could serve as wings—feathers, paper, silk. "I am going to begin my paper wings tomorrow," she wrote to her mother, who was traveling abroad. She signed the letter "Your very affectionate carrier pigeon."

Like all good scientists, Ada needed to keep a record of her findings. She created a book, which she titled *Flyology*, and festooned it with drawings of all her experiments. On the final page, she included her design for a steam-powered mechanical flying horse.

BEHOLD, THE MODERN PEGASUS!

"This last scheme probably has infinitely more difficulties and obstacles in its way than my scheme for flying," Ada admitted in another letter to her mother, "but still I should think that it is possible."

Lady Byron didn't approve of her daughter's flights of fancy. When she returned home, she reprimanded Ada for neglecting her studies and ordered her to discontinue her experiments. A short time later, Ada contracted a bad case of measles and was confined to her bed for several years. The steam-powered horse never got built.

Though illness put her plans on hold, Ada never lost her passion for poetical science. When she was seventeen, she attended a party at the home of Charles Babbage, a famous mathematician and inventor. After an evening of dancing and games, Babbage took Ada aside and showed her his latest invention. The Difference Engine was a two-ton, hand-cranked calculating machine that could solve complex mathematical problems.

The machine was one of the world's first computers. Ada, with her mathematical mind and romantic imagination, immediately fell in love with it. She wrote to Babbage requesting the blueprints for the Difference Engine so she could better understand how it worked. The two became pen pals. Babbage was so impressed by Ada's suggestions for improvements that he gave her the nickname the Enchantress of Numbers.

Ada came to the conclusion that Babbage's machine "might act upon other things besides numbers," such as music, sound, text, and pictures. In effect, she had envisioned the future in which modern computers help us do everything from composing songs to creating cartoons. As one of Ada's biographers said, "she saw the poetry in such an idea, and she set out to encourage others to see it as well."

For these breakthroughs, as well as for her effort to write coded instructions that could be carried out by a machine, Ada Lovelace is sometimes called the mother of computer programming. Many years after her death, the U.S. Department of Defense recognized her achievements by naming a programming language after her.

Ada Lovelace Day, held every year on the second Tuesday of October, celebrates the contributions of women to science, technology, engineering, and math. None of that would have been possible were it not for Ada Lovelace, the poetical scientist and enchantress of numbers.

IT'S NOT AS COOL AS MY FLYING HORSE, BUT IT'S STILL PRETTY GREAT.

Nikola Tesla

Like Mother, Like Son

The "mad scientist" who brought neon lights and AC power to the world was born in the middle of an electrical storm. Inspired by his mother's example, Nikola Tesla used his scientific genius—and his head for solving problems—to earn a place in the history books as one of the world's most creative inventors.

On a rainy summer night in 1856, in the small village of Smiljan in present-day Croatia, Djuka Tesla gave birth to her second son and the fourth of her five children. Nikola Tesla took his first breaths just as a bolt of lightning struck.

"Your new son is a child of the storm," remarked the nurse who helped deliver him. No, Djuka replied:

Nikki, as he came to be called, was born into a brilliant and distinguished family. His father, Milutin, was an Eastern Orthodox priest who knew the entire Bible by heart. His older brother Dane was considered a boy genius and was expected to one day bring fame and honor to the Tesla family.

But the person Nikki took after the most was his mother. She spoke four languages, despite never learning to read or write. Djuka's father and grandfather were inventors, and she followed their example. She used her ingenuity to invent small appliances and useful contraptions to help in her work around the house as well as the care of her family.

When the children complained about the amount of effort it took to climb onto their high four-poster beds, she designed a bed without legs that was much easier to get into. When they bemoaned their lack of privacy, she devised a screen with hinges that separated their beds from one another.

Fed up with scrambling eggs by hand, Djuka also created a mechanical egg beater out of a pair of wooden forks tied together with string. But the device made her wrists ache from the constant churning. If only she could find a way to power it, she lamented, then she'd really get somewhere.

Through it all, young Nikki looked on, wondering if he could figure out a way to improve his mother's inventions. Someday, he thought, he would come up with a way to power that egg beater!

When Nikki was five, Dane was killed in a horse riding accident. Nikki was now the oldest boy in the Tesla family, and he was expected to follow in his older brother's footsteps. In the aftermath of the tragedy, he vowed to be as good and as smart as Dane had been, bringing honor to the family name. But how?

The more he thought about it, the more Nikki felt that inventing things was his ticket to fame and fortune. He started small, fashioning his first inventions out of everyday objects. He carved swords from scraps of wooden furniture. When he had one carved to his liking, he headed into a nearby cornfield and spent hours "mowing down my enemies in the form of corn-stalks." But there was a downside: he ruined the year's corn crop and earned a severe scolding from his mother.

Next, Nikki set his sights on a more practical invention. One day, when he was playing outside with some friends, a boy showed up with a hook and fishing tackle. Nikki was excited at the prospect of using it to catch frogs. But then he got into a fight with the boy who owned the gear and was disinvited from the fishing expedition. The other boys trundled off to the creek without him.

Left to his own devices, Nikki decided to make his own fishhook. He found a piece of iron wire, hammered the end to a sharp point using two stones, and fastened it to a sturdy string. Then he cut a rod, gathered some bait, and headed down to the creek. There he found a frog sitting placidly on a stump.

Nikki dangled the hook in front of the frog. The curious creature's eyes bulged in anticipation. Puffing up to twice its normal size, the frog made a sudden snap at the bait. The second the frog bit down, Nikki reeled it in.

It was the first of many frogs Nikki caught that day, to the amazement of his friends, who had returned from their trip empty-handed.

For a while, Nikki kept his invention secret. But when his anger had cooled, he let them use it too. "The following summer brought disaster to the frogs," he later wrote.

Nikki had won the respect of his friends and seemed well on his way to establishing himself as the town's resident inventor. But an unlucky accident threatened to turn the people of Smiljan against him.

Nikki had taken a job as the bell ringer in church. One Sunday, after services were over, Nikki hurried down from the belfry and accidentally stepped on the gown of the wealthiest lady in town.

"It tore off with a ripping noise which sounded like a salvo of musketry," Nikki later remembered. After she gathered up her tattered train, the outraged woman demanded that Nikki be punished. Nikki's father was reluctant to do so, but the townspeople had already judged him reckless and irresponsible. It would take a heroic feat for Nikki to regain their favor.

A short time later, such an opportunity arose. The citizens of Smiljan had raised money to buy a new fire engine, and the entire town came out to see its unveiling. When the ceremony was complete, the city leaders gave the order to pump water through the mighty hose. The crowd held their breath in anticipation, but not a drop of water squirted from the nozzle. A group of professors came forward, but they could not determine the cause of the trouble.

With nothing to lose, Nikki pushed to the head of the crowd. "I can fix it!" he declared, and he proceeded to feel around for the point where the suction hose had collapsed, choking off the water supply.

In a few seconds, Nikki had opened it up and the water rushed forth in a torrent, drenching some of the onlookers. But no one minded. They were so happy to have their fire engine in working order, they lifted Nikki on their shoulders and carried him through the town square in triumph.

Nikki's quick thinking had won the respect of his neighbors, but he still had one piece of unfinished business to take care of. He was determined to come up with a way to power his mother's egg beater.

The more he thought about it, however, the more impossible it seemed. Then one day, Nikki was playing with his pet dog by the creek when an idea occurred to him. What if he could harness the power of running water and use it to turn the gears of the egg beater?

Nikki spent the next few years perfecting what he called his "water wheel," an early example of what would later be known as a "Tesla Turbine." The gadget generated power, but Nikki knew he could do better. Once again, he found inspiration in the world of nature.

After watching junebugs fly around his yard on a summer day, Nikki began to wonder about their ability to stay aloft for long periods. He caught four of them in a net, and then glued one to each blade of a homemade propeller. When the bugs beat their wings, they caused the propeller to turn. To Nikki's amazement, they whirled for hours and never seemed to get tired.

THIS IS FUN.

I'M GETTING DIZZY . . .

WHEEEEE!

Just as Nikki was about to declare his experiment a success, one of his neighbors dropped by. The boy had an appetite for insects—and an appalling lack of table manners. One by one, he plucked the bugs off Nikki's propeller and popped them into his mouth.

Nikki was repulsed. "That disgusting sight terminated my endeavors in this promising field," he remembered later. He never touched a junebug again, "or any other insect for that matter."

When he was fourteen, Nikki left home to attend high school in the faraway town of Karlovac. He was determined to become an engineer, but his father was dead set against the idea. "One inventor in this family is enough!" he declared, urging Nikki to study for the priesthood instead.

After completing high school, Nikki returned home. He hoped to persuade his father to change his mind. Shortly after he arrived, however, he contracted cholera.

He was confined to his bed for nine months and nearly died. Mr. Tesla was so distraught that he made a promise to send him to the best engineering school in the land if he recovered.

Milutin Tesla may not have been thrilled by his son's career choice, but he was a man of his word. As soon as Nikki recovered, he allowed his son to attend university on an engineering scholarship. Although Nikola Tesla never did complete his formal schooling, his inventive spirit could not be contained. Among the many creations he ushered into the world were the X-ray photo, AC power, radio waves, neon lights, radar detection, remote control, and the bladeless turbine.

Stephen Hawking

The Boy Builder

Even the greatest geniuses start out small. Stephen Hawking went from building balsa wood airplanes at his friend's house to mapping out the universe with a supercomputer. His life-long fascination with the way things work helped turn him into one of the world's most brilliant theoretical physicists.

"I am just a child that has never grown up," Stephen Hawking once wrote. "I still keep asking these how and why questions. Occasionally I find an answer."

Stephen's search for answers began in the English village of Highgate, a suburb of London. While he was growing up, World War II was raging, and the British capital was subjected to almost daily bombings by German airplanes—a campaign of destruction known as the Blitz.

One day, a German rocket landed just a few houses away from where Stephen lived. He wasn't home at the time, but later he got to survey the damage and play in the rubble with his friends.

Highgate was home to many prominent scientists, and Stephen's father was one of them. He worked as a medical researcher specializing in the study of tropical diseases. Stephen's mother was one of the first female students to graduate from Oxford University. Both of his parents placed a high value on education. But young Stephen did not—at least not yet.

When he was two and a half years old, Stephen's parents sent him to school. On the first day of class, he stood up in the middle of the room and began to cry. And he did not stop until his parents arrived to bring him home.

After that incident, Stephen didn't return to school for a year and a half. When he finally did go back, he showed little interest in schoolwork. In fact, he disliked studying so much that he didn't learn to read until he was eight years old.

Stephen may not have been a fan of school, but he always enjoying learning about things on his own.

As a young boy, he developed a passion for model trains. His father built a train set for him out of wood, but Stephen wasn't happy with it. He wanted one that moved by its own power.

I NEED TO STUDY HOW TRAINS WORK.

So Stephen's father tried again. That Christmas, he gave his son a second-hand mechanical train, which he had repaired himself. You could wind it up with a key to make it go, but it didn't work very well.

He tried yet again. After the end of World War II, Mr. Hawking traveled to the United States on business. He returned with a glittering new mechanical train, complete with a figure-eight track. But Stephen still dreamed of an electric train . . .

Stephen saved his money for years and finally had enough. He waited until his parents were away and then withdrew his entire savings from the bank. All the money Stephen had been given for birthdays and special occasions barely added up to the cost of a new electric train set. But he had just enough.

There was only one small problem—it didn't work! Even after Stephen scraped together even more money to have the motor repaired, the train still never ran very well. But he had learned a valuable lesson: if you want something to work properly, you have to build it yourself.

When Stephen was eight years old, his family moved to a town north of London called St. Albans, where his father had taken a job. At first, Stephen was excited to be moving into a new home. But then he got a look at the place.

The house had once been an opulent mansion, but now it was a broken-down wreck with peeling wall-paper, holes in the walls, and cracked windows every-where. Since Mr. Hawking's new position didn't pay very much, his parents were unable to pay for repairs. When a piece of furniture wore out, they just let it fall apart. There was no central heating system, so the family had to wear sweaters all the time to keep warm.

Mr. Hawking couldn't afford to buy a new car, so instead he purchased a used taxicab and asked Stephen to help him build a makeshift garage using prefabri-cated steel. When the neighbors saw what they were driving, and how they were living, they were aghast. The family soon became known as the town eccentrics.

Stephen's new classmates didn't quite know what to make of him, either. Small and uncoordinated, Stephen dressed poorly and was bad at sports. He spoke very fast, in a garbled manner that his classmates dubbed "Hawkingese." He had a strange way of hiccupping when he laughed, almost choking with every chuckle.

In the classroom, Stephen was far from the brilliant student he would one day become. "My handwriting was bad, and I could be lazy," he later admitted. At the end of the year, he finished third from the bottom of his class. One of his classmates even bet a bag of candy that Stephen would never amount to anything.

Fed up with being underestimated, Stephen worked hard to turn his reputation around. He began hanging out with other outsiders who shared his passion for building things. He made friends with a boy named John McClenahan, whose father had a workshop in his house. He and Stephen spent hours constructing model airplanes out of balsa wood.

STEPHEN, THESE PLANS ARE PRETTY COMPLEX.

WE CAN DO IT!

Tired of playing children's games like Candyland and Uncle Wiggily, Stephen joined forces with another of his friends, Roger Ferneyhough, and together they began inventing their own. Stephen came up with the rules, and Roger designed the boards and pieces. Their masterpiece was an alaborate medieval war game, complete with laws, treaties, budgets, and armies.

For Stephen, making things was like creating his own universe, one that he alone controlled. He became an expert at taking stuff apart, like clocks and radios, although he was not as good at putting them back together. One time he attempted to transform an old television set into an amplifier. But when he plugged it in, he found himself on the receiving end of a 500-volt electric shock.

Failed experiments were few and far between, however. Before long, the same kids who had once bet against Stephen had grown to respect him. They even gave him a new nickname: "Einstein."

Around this same time, Stephen began to accompany his father to his job at the National Institute for Medica Research. In his laboratory, Mr. Hawking was studying tropical diseases. Together they visited the insect house, which was filled with mosquitos carrying the deadly disease malaria.

Stephen was increasingly fascinated by the world of science. But while his father hoped that he would study medicine or biology, Stephen wanted to chart a different course. As he later wrote: "The brightest boys did mathematics and physics."

It was at St. Alban's that Stephen was introduced to the wonders of math, which his teacher Dikran Tahta called "the blueprint of the universe." That idea appealed to Stephen, who had always been interested in how things were built and designed.

Unlike the classes of most of Stephen's teachers, his math lessons were lively and exciting. Stephen later credited Mr. Tahta with inspiring him to become a professor of mathematics. "Behind every exceptional person, there is an exceptional teacher," he wrote.

Mr. Tahta was also the guiding force behind Stephen's most ambitious project yet. When Stephen was sixteen, shortly before he left for Oxford University, he and his friends decided to construct their own computer. They planned to use recycled clock parts, an old telephone switchboard, and other odds and ends.

It took them a month to get the creaky machine to work, but with a little extra soldering, and a lot of combined brainpower, they were able to patch it together. They called it the Logical Uniselector Computing Engine, or LUCE for short.

Eventually the boys were able to program the computer to solve basic math problems. Their achievement drew the attention of the townspeople, and they were written about in the local newspaper. It was the first of many scientific breakthroughs for which Stephen would be celebrated.

After Stephen left the school, the new computer teacher discovered a box of metal parts and wires. Thinking it was junk, he threw it all in the trash. Only many years later did he discover that the box of scraps was part of Stephen's great boyhood invention, LUCE.

Stephen Hawking developed ground-breaking theories about black holes, the nature of gravity, and the origin of the universe. He achieved these and many other accomplishments despite having a severe disability called amyotrophic lateral sclerosis (ALS), which he contracted when he was 21 years old. But nothing would stop him from seeking answers to puzzling questions and becoming one of the most respected scientists in the world.

* * *

TRY AS WE MIGHT, WE COULDN'T FIT

EVERY

Kid Scientist

INTO

ONE

BOOK.

HERE ARE SOME

FUN
FACTS

ABOUT OTHER FAMOUS SCIENTISTS

YOU MAY HAVE HEARD ABOUT.

Astronomer **CARL SAGAN'S** interest in outer space was sparked when he read about the interplanetary adventures of John Carter of Mars, a character created by author Edgar Rice Burroughs.

||||||||||||||||||||||||||||||||||||||||||||||||||||||||||||||||||||||||||||||||||||||||||||||||||||||||||||||||

Paleontologist **MARY LEAKEY** was expelled from school twice—once for refusing to recite poetry, and once for blowing up the chemistry lab.

||||||||||||||||||||||||||||||||||||||||||||||||||||||||||||||||||||||||||||||||||||||||||||||||||||||||||||||||

French mathematician **SOPHIE GERMAIN'S** parents so disapproved of her fascination with numbers that they denied her warm clothes and a fire to study by. Every night, she lit candles, wrapped herself in quilts, and did her calculations in secret.

||||||||||||||||||||||||||||||||||||||||||||||||||||||||||||||||||||||||||||||||||||||||||||||||||||||||||||||||

Computer scientist **ALAN TURING** was a poor student who was always getting into trouble at school. One of his teachers called his handwriting "the worst I have ever seen." The school headmaster wrote that he was "the sort of boy who is bound to be a problem for any school or community."

||||||||||||||||||||||||||||||||||||||||||||||||||||||||||||||||||||||||||||||||||||||||||||||||||||||||||||||||

GALILEO was a true Renaissance man. As a boy, he mastered the lute, a stringed instrument popular in 16th century Italy.

|||||||||||||||||||||||||||||||||||||||||||||||||||||||||||||||||||||||||||||||||||||||||||||||||||||||||||||||||||||||||

When he was eleven, physicist RICHARD FEYNMAN built a burglar alarm out of a battery and a bell connected by wire. He hung it from his bedroom door so it would go off whenever his parents tried to enter his room.

|||||||||||||||||||||||||||||||||||||||||||||||||||||||||||||||||||||||||||||||||||||||||||||||||||||||||||||||||||||||||

The first woman in the United States to receive a medical degree, ELIZABETH BLACKWELL grew up in a family of staunch abolitionists. As a girl, she and her parents helped escaping slaves during the Civil War by hiding them in their home.

|||||||||||||||||||||||||||||||||||||||||||||||||||||||||||||||||||||||||||||||||||||||||||||||||||||||||||||||||||||||||

SOFIA KOVALEVSKAYA, the first woman to receive a doctorate in mathematics, papered over the walls of her childhood bedroom with calculus notes.

|||||||||||||||||||||||||||||||||||||||||||||||||||||||||||||||||||||||||||||||||||||||||||||||||||||||||||||||||||||||||

As a high school student, physicist MICHIO KAU built his own particle accelerator in the family garage.

|||||||||||||||||||||||||||||||||||||||||||||||||||||||||||||||||||||||||||||||||||||||||||||||||||||||||||||||||||||||||

Microbiologist BARBARA McCLINTOCK'S birth name was Eleanor. Her parents changed her name to Barbara when she was a young girl because they thought Eleanor sounded "too feminine."

||||||||||||||||||||||||||||||||||||||||||||||||||||||||||||||||||||||||||||||||||||||||||||||||||||||||||

DIAN FOSSEY became famous for studying gorillas. But she first developed her love of animals as a young girl, when she cared for a pet goldfish.

||||||||||||||||||||||||||||||||||||||||||||||||||||||||||||||||||||||||||||||||||||||||||||||||||||||||||

Astronomer EDWIN HUBBLE received his first telescope on his eighth birthday. He was so excited that he skipped his own party to study the stars from his bedroom window.

||||||||||||||||||||||||||||||||||||||||||||||||||||||||||||||||||||||||||||||||||||||||||||||||||||||||||

STEPHEN JAY GOULD decided to become a paleontologist when he was five years old after a visit to the Hall of Dinosaurs at New York's Museum of Natural History.

||||||||||||||||||||||||||||||||||||||||||||||||||||||||||||||||||||||||||||||||||||||||||||||||||||||||||

When he was twelve, aspiring electrical engineer JOHN AMBROSE FLEMING built his own camera out of a cigar box and a magnifying glass.

||||||||||||||||||||||||||||||||||||||||||||||||||||||||||||||||||||||||||||||||||||||||||||||||||||||||||

Paleontologist **MARY ANNING** survived being struck by lightning when she was just fifteen months old.

||||||||||||||||||||||||||||||||||||||||||||||||||||||||||||||||||||||||||||||||||||||||||||||||||||||

Statistician and nursing pioneer **FLORENCE NIGHTINGALE** loved cats and had numerous pets including a pig, a donkey, and a pony.

||||||||||||||||||||||||||||||||||||||||||||||||||||||||||||||||||||||||||||||||||||||||||||||||||||||

Ornithologist **SALIM ALI**, often called "the Birdman of India," got his start by adopting baby sparrows as a boy. When he couldn't successfully toilet train one, he asked his mother to knit a pair of diapers for it.

||||||||||||||||||||||||||||||||||||||||||||||||||||||||||||||||||||||||||||||||||||||||||||||||||||||

Astronaut **MAE JEMISON**, the first woman of color to travel in space, was inspired by the character of Lieutenant Uhura on the television series *Star Trek*.

||||||||||||||||||||||||||||||||||||||||||||||||||||||||||||||||||||||||||||||||||||||||||||||||||||||

Further Reading

DO YOU
KNOW WHERE
THE CHEESE
SECTION IS?

Bibliography

There are many great books about great scientists, including autobiographies (books written by the person about himself or herself) and biographies (books about noteworthy people written by someone else). This is a list of main sources used by the author in researching and writing this book.

PART ONE

Reaching for the Stars

Katherine Johnson

Feldman, Thea. *You Should Meet: Katherine Johnson.* Simon Spotlight, 2017.

Shetterly, Margot Lee. *Hidden Figures.* William Morrow, 2016.

Vera Rubin

Bartusiak, Marcia. *Through a Universe Darkly.* HarperCollins, 1993.

Sally Ride

Mattern, Joanne. *Sally Ride: Astronaut.* Infobase, 2006.

Sherr, Lynn. *Sally Ride: America's First Woman in Space.* Simon & Schuster, 2014.

Neil deGrasse Tyson

Tyson, Neil deGrasse. *The Sky Is Not the Limit.* Prometheus Books, 2004.

Ventura, Marne. *Neil deGrasse Tyson: Astrophysicist and Space Advocate.* Lerner Publications, 2014.

PART TWO

Green Thumbs and Animal Lovers

George Washington Carver

Abrams, Dennis. *George Washington Carver: Scientist and Educator.* Infobase Publishing, 2008.

Moore, Eva. *The Story of George Washington Carver.* Scholastic, 1971.

Rachel Carson

Lear, Linda. *Rachel Carson: Witness for Nature.* Henry Holt, 1997.

Souder, William. *On a Farther Shore: The Life and Legacy of Rachel Carson.* Crown, 2012.

Jane Goodall

Goodall, Jane. *Reason for Hope: A Spiritual Journey.* Warner Books, 1999.

Greene, Meg. *Jane Goodall: A Biography*. Prometheus Books, 2008.

Peterson, Dale. *Jane Goodall: The Woman Who Redefined Man*. Mariner Books, 2006.

Temple Grandin

Cutler, Eustacia. *A Thorn in My Pocket: Temple Grandin's Mother Tells the Family Story*. Future Horizons, 2004.

Wood, Annette. *Temple Grandin: Voice for the Voiceless*. Skyhorse, 2016.

PART THREE

The Invisible Forces

Isaac Newton

Ackroyd, Peter. *Newton*. Doubleday, 2006.

Iliffe, Rob. *Newton: A Very Short Introduction*. Oxford University Press, 2007.

Marie Curie

Curie, Eve. *Madame Curie: A Biography*. Da Capo Press, 2001.

Krull, Kathleen. *Marie Curie*. Puffin, 2007.

Reid, Robert. *Marie Curie*. New American Library, 1974.

Albert Einstein

McPherson, Stephanie Sammartino. *Ordinary Genius: The Story of Albert Einstein*. Lerner Books, 1995.

Severance, John B. *Einstein: Visionary Scientist*. Clarion Books, 1999.

Rosalind Franklin

Glynn, Jenifer. *My Sister Rosalind Franklin*. Oxford University Press, 2012.

Maddox, Brenda. *Rosalind Franklin: The Dark Lady of DNA*. HarperCollins, 2002.

PART FOUR

Do It Yourself

Benjamin Franklin

Higgins, Maria Mihalik. *Benjamin Franklin: Revolutionary Inventor*. Sterling, 2007.

Isaacson, Walter. *Benjamin Franklin: An American Life*. Simon and Schuster, 2003.

Ada Lovelace

Essinger, James. *Ada's Algorithm: How Lord Byron's Daughter Ada Lovelace Launched the Digital Age*. Melville House, 2014.

Lethbridge, Lucy. *Ada Lovelace: The Computer Wizard of Victorian*

Nikola Tesla

Tesla, Nikola. *My Inventions: The Autobiography of Nikola Tesla.* Merchant Books, 2013.

Stephen Hawking

Hawking, Stephen. *My Brief History.* Bantam Books, 2013.

White, Michael and Dr. John Gribbin. *Stephen Hawking: A Life in Science.* Pegasus Books, 2016.

GENERAL INTEREST

Ignotofsky, Rachel. *Women in Science.* Ten Speed Press, 2016.

Swaby, Rachel. *Headstrong: 52 Women Who Changed Science—and the World.* Broadway Books, 2015.

Index

They're Little Kids with Big Dreams . . . and Big Problems!

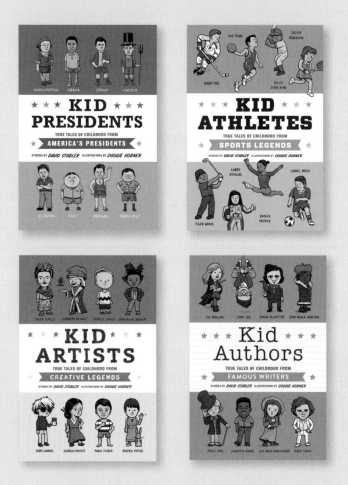